State of Vermont
Department of Libraries
Midstate Regional Library
RFD #4
Montpelier, Vt. 05602
WIT

City Life

Also by Donald Barthelme

COME BACK, DR. CALIGARI

SNOW WHITE

UNSPEAKABLE PRACTICES, UNNATURAL ACTS

City Life

Donald Barthelme

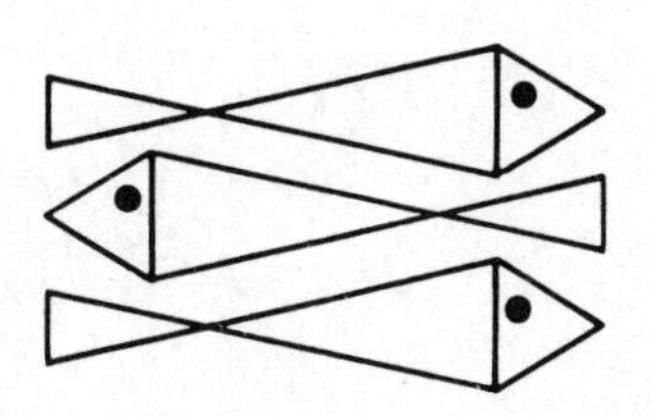

Farrar, Straus & Giroux New York

Copyright © 1968, 1969, 1970 by Donald Barthelme
All rights reserved
Library of Congress catalog card number: 74-113775
Published simultaneously in Canada
by Doubleday Canada, Ltd., Toronto
Printed in the United States of America
Third printing, 1975
Designed by Patricia de Groot

Except for "Bone Bubbles" and "The Glass Mountain," all the stories in this book appeared originally in *The New Yorker*. The author is grateful to *The New Yorker* for permission to reprint.

The author also wishes to thank *The Paris Review* for permission to reprint "Bone Bubbles."

To Roger Angell

Contents

Views of My Father Weeping

An aristocrat was riding down the street in his carriage. He ran over my father.

•

After the ceremony I walked back to the city. I was trying to think of the reason my father had died. Then I remembered: he was run over by a carriage.

•

I telephoned my mother and told her of my father's death. She said she supposed it was the best thing. I too supposed it was the best thing. His enjoyment was diminishing. I wondered if I should attempt to trace the aristocrat whose carriage had run him down. There were said to have been one or two witnesses.

•

Yes it is possible that it is not my father who sits there in the center of the bed weeping. It may be someone else, the mailman, the man who delivers the groceries, an insurance salesman or tax collector, who knows. However, I must say, it resembles my father. The resemblance is very strong. He is not smiling through his tears but frowning through them. I remember once we were out on the ranch shooting peccadillos (result of a meeting, on the plains of the West, of the collared peccary and the nine-banded armadillo). My father shot and missed. He wept. This weeping resembles that weeping.

•

"Did you see it?" "Yes but only part of it. Part of the time I had my back turned." The witness was a little girl, eleven or twelve. She lived in a very poor quarter and I could not imagine that, were she to testify, anyone would credit her. "Can you recall what the man in the carriage looked like?" "Like an aristocrat," she said.

•

The first witness declares that the man in the carriage looked "like an aristocrat." But that might be simply the carriage itself. Any man sitting in a handsome carriage with a driver on the box and perhaps one or two footmen up behind tends to look like an aristocrat. I wrote down her name and asked her to call me if she remembered anything else. I gave her some candy.

•

I stood in the square where my father was killed and asked people passing by if they had seen, or knew of anyone who had seen, the incident. At the same time I felt the effort was wasted. Even if I found the man whose carriage had done the job, what would I say to him? "You killed my father." "Yes," the aristocrat would say, "but he ran right in under the legs of the horses. My man tried to stop but it happened too quickly. There was nothing anyone could do." Then perhaps he would offer me a purse full of money.

•

The man sitting in the center of the bed looks very much like my father. He is weeping, tears coursing down his cheeks. One can see that he is upset about something. Looking at him I see that something is wrong. He is spewing like a fire hydrant with its lock knocked off. His yammer darts in and out of all the rooms. In a melting mood I lay my paw on my breast and say, "Father." This does not distract him from his plaint, which rises to a shriek, sinks to a pule. His range is great, his ambition commensurate. I say again, "Father," but he ignores me. I don't know whether it is time to flee or will not be time to flee until later. He may suddenly stop, assume a sternness. I have kept the door open and nothing between me and the door, and moreover the screen unlatched, and on top of that the motor running, in the Mustang. But perhaps it is not my father weeping there, but another father: Tom's father, Phil's father, Pat's father, Pete's father, Paul's father. Apply some sort of test, voiceprint reading or

•

My father throws his ball of knitting up in the air. The orange wool hangs there.

•

My father regards the tray of pink cupcakes. Then he jams his thumb into each cupcake, into the top. Cupcake by cupcake. A thick smile spreads over the face of each cupcake.

•

Then a man volunteered that he had heard two other men talking about the accident in a shop. "What shop?" The man pointed it out to me, a draper's shop on the south side of the square. I entered the shop and made inquiries. "It was your father, eh? He was bloody clumsy if you ask me." This was the clerk behind the counter. But another man standing nearby, well-dressed, even elegant, a gold watchchain stretched across his vest, disagreed. "It was the fault of the driver," the second man said. "He could have stopped them if he had cared to." "Nonsense," the clerk said, "not a chance in the world. If your father hadn't been drunk—" "He wasn't drunk," I said. "I arrived on the scene soon after it happened and I smelled no liquor."

•

This was true. I had been notified by the police, who came to my room and fetched me to the scene of the accident. I bent over my father, whose chest was crushed, and laid my cheek against his. His cheek was cold. I smelled no liquor but blood from his mouth stained the collar of my coat. I asked the people standing there how it had happened. "Run down by a carriage," they said. "Did the driver stop?" "No, he whipped up the horses and went off down the street and then around the corner at the end of the street, toward King's New Square." "You have no idea as to whose carriage . . ." "None." Then I made the arrangements for the burial. It was not until several days later that the idea of seeking the aristocrat in the carriage came to me.

•

I had had in my life nothing to do with aristocrats, did not even know in what part of the city they lived, in their great houses. So that even if I located someone who had seen the incident and could identify the particular aristocrat involved, I would be faced with the further task of finding his house and gaining admittance (and even then, might he not be abroad?). "No, the driver was at fault," the man with the gold watchchain said. "Even if your father was drunk—and I can't say about that, one way or another, I have no opinion —even if your father was drunk, the driver could have done more to avoid the accident. He was dragged, you know. The carriage dragged him about forty feet." I had noticed that my father's clothes were torn in a peculiar way. "There was one thing," the clerk said, "don't tell anyone I told you, but I can give you one hint. The driver's livery was blue and green."

•

It is someone's father. That much is clear. He is fatherly. The gray in the head. The puff in the face. The droop in the shoulders. The flab on the gut. Tears falling. Tears falling. Tears falling. Tears falling. More tears. It seems that he intends to go further along this salty path. The facts suggest that this is his program, weeping. He has something in mind, more weeping. O lud lud! But why remain? Why watch it? Why tarry? Why not fly? Why subject myself? I could be somewhere else, reading a book, watching the telly, stuffing a big ship into a little bottle, dancing the Pig. I could be out in the streets feeling up eleven-year-old girls in their soldier drag, there are thousands, as alike as pennies, and I could be— Why doesn't he stand up, arrange his clothes, dry his face? He's trying to embarrass us. He wants attention. He's trying to make himself interesting. He wants his brow wrapped in cold cloths perhaps, his hands held perhaps, his back rubbed, his neck kneaded, his wrists patted, his elbows anointed with rare oils, his toenails painted with tiny scenes representing God blessing America. I won't do it.

•

My father has a red bandana tied around his face covering the nose and mouth. He extends his right hand in which there is a water pistol. "Stick 'em up!" he says.

•

But blue and green livery is not unusual. A blue coat with green trousers, or the reverse, if I saw a coachman wearing such livery I would take no particular notice. It is true that most livery tends to be blue and buff, or blue and white, or blue and a sort of darker blue (for the trousers). But in these days one often finds a servant aping the more exquisite color combinations affected by his masters. I have even seen them in red trousers although red trousers used to be reserved, by unspoken agreement, for the aristocracy. So that the colors of the driver's livery were not of much consequence. Still it was something. I could now go about in the city, especially in stables and gin shops and such places, keeping a weather eye for the livery of the lackeys who gathered there. It was possible that more than one of the gentry dressed his servants in this blue and green livery, but on the other hand, unlikely that there were as many as half a dozen. So that in fact the draper's clerk had offered a very good clue indeed, had one the energy to pursue it vigorously.

•

There is my father, standing alongside an extremely large dog, a dog ten hands high at the very least. My father leaps on the dog's back, straddles him. My father kicks the large dog in the ribs with his heels. "Giddyap!"

•

My father has written on the white wall with his crayons.

•

I was stretched out on my bed when someone knocked at the door. It was the small girl to whom I had given candy when I had first begun searching for the aristocrat. She looked frightened, yet resolute; I could see that she had some information for me. "I know who it was," she said. "I know his name." "What is it?" "First you must give me five crowns." Luckily I had five crowns in my pocket; had she come later in the day, after I had eaten, I would have had nothing to give her. I handed over the money and she said, "Lars Bang." I looked at her in some surprise. "What sort of name is that for an aristocrat?" "His coachman," she said. "The coachman's name is Lars Bang." Then she fled.

•

When I heard this name, which in its sound and appearance is rude, vulgar, not unlike my own name, I was seized with repugnance, thought of dropping the whole business, although the piece of information she had brought had just cost me five crowns. When I was seeking him and he was yet nameless, the aristocrat and, by extension, his servants, seemed vulnerable: they had, after all, been responsible for a crime, or a sort of crime. My father was dead and they were responsible, or at least involved; and even though they were of the aristocracy or servants of the aristocracy, still common justice might be sought for; they might be required to make reparation, in some measure, for what they had done. Now, having the name of the coachman, and being thus much closer to his master than when I merely had the clue of the blue and green livery, I became afraid. For, after all, the unknown aristocrat must be a very powerful man, not at all accustomed to being called to account by people like me; indeed, his contempt for people like me was so great that, when one of us was so foolish as to stray into the path of his carriage, the aristocrat dashed him down, or permitted his coachman to do so, dragged him along the cobblestones for as much as forty feet, and then went gaily on his way, toward King's New Square. Such a man, I reasoned, was not very likely to take kindly to what I had to say to him. Very possibly there would be no purse of money at all, not a crown, not an öre; but rather he would, with an abrupt, impatient nod of his head, set his servants upon me. I would be beaten, perhaps killed. Like my father.

•

But if it is not my father sitting there in the bed weeping, why am I standing before the bed, in an attitude of supplication? Why do I desire with all my heart that this man, my father, cease what he is doing, which is so painful to me? Is it only that my position is a familiar one? That I remember, before, desiring with all my heart that this man, my father, cease what he is doing?

•

Why! . . . there's my father! . . . sitting in the bed there! . . . and he's *weeping!* . . . as though his heart would burst! . . . Father! . . . how is this? . . . who has wounded you? . . . name the man! . . . why I'll . . . I'll . . . here, Father, take this handkerchief! . . . and this handkerchief! . . . and this handkerchief! . . . I'll run for a towel . . . for a doctor . . . for a priest . . . for a good fairy . . . is there . . . can you . . . can I . . . a cup of hot tea? . . . bowl of steaming soup? . . . shot of Calvados? . . . a joint? . . . a red jacket? . . . a blue jacket? . . . Father, please! . . . look at me, Father . . . who has insulted you? . . . are you, then, compromised? . . . ruined? . . . a slander is going around? . . . an obloquy? . . . a traducement? . . . 'sdeath! . . . I won't permit it! . . . I won't abide it! . . . I'll . . . move every mountain . . . climb . . . every river . . . etc.

•

My father is playing with the salt and pepper shakers, and with the sugar bowl. He lifts the cover off the sugar bowl, and shakes pepper into it.

•

Or: My father thrusts his hand through a window of the doll's house. His hand knocks over the doll's chair, knocks over the doll's chest of drawers, knocks over the doll's bed.

•

The next day, just before noon, Lars Bang himself came to my room. "I understand that you are looking for me." He was very much of a surprise. I had expected a rather burly, heavy man, of a piece with all of the other coachmen one saw sitting up on the box; Lars Bang was, instead, slight, almost feminine-looking, more the type of the secretary or valet than the coachman. He was not threatening at all, contrary to my fears; he was almost helpful, albeit with the slightest hint of malice in his helpfulness. I stammeringly explained that my father, a good man although subject to certain weaknesses, including a love of the bottle, had been run down by an aristocrat's coach, in the vicinity of King's New Square, not very many days previously; that I had information that the coach had dragged him some forty feet; and that I was eager to establish certain facts about the case. "Well then," Lars Bang said, with a helpful nod, "I'm your man, for it was my coach that was involved. A sorry business! Unfortunately I haven't the time right now to give you the full particulars, but if you will call round at the address written on this card, at six o'clock in the evening, I believe I will be able to satisfy you." So saying, he took himself off, leaving me with the card in my hand.

•

I spoke to Miranda, quickly sketching what had happened. She asked to see the white card; I gave it to her, for the address meant nothing to me. "Oh my," she said. "17 rue du Bac, that's over by the Vixen Gate—a very special quarter. Only aristocrats of the highest rank live there, and common people are not even allowed into the great park that lies between the houses and the river. If you are found wandering about there at night, you are apt to earn yourself a very severe beating." "But I have an appointment," I said. "An appointment with a coachman!" Miranda cried, "how foolish you are! Do you think the men of the watch will believe that, or even if they believe it (you have an honest enough face) will allow you to prowl that rich quarter, where so many thieves would dearly love to be set free for an hour or so, after dark? Go to!" Then she advised me that I must carry something with me, a pannier of beef or some dozen bottles of wine, so that if apprehended by the watch, I could say that I was delivering to such and such a house, and thus be judged an honest man on an honest errand, and escape a beating. I saw that she was right; and going out, I purchased at the wine merchant's a dozen bottles of a rather good claret (for it would never do to be delivering wine no aristocrat would drink); this cost me thirty crowns, which I had borrowed from Miranda. The bottles we wrapped round with straw, to prevent them banging into one another, and the whole we arranged in a sack, which I could carry on my back. I remember thinking, how they rhymed, fitted together, *sack* and *back*. In this fashion I set off across the city.

•

There is my father's bed. In it, my father. Attitude of dejection. Graceful as a mule deer once, the same large ears. For a nanosecond, there is a nanosmile. Is he having me on? I remember once we went out on the ups and downs of the West (out past Vulture's Roost) to shoot. First we shot up a lot of old beer cans, then we shot up a lot of old whiskey bottles, better because they shattered. Then we shot up some mesquite bushes and some parts of a Ford pickup somebody'd left lying around. But no animals came to our party (it was noisy, I admit it). A long list of animals failed to arrive, no deer, quail, rabbit, seals, sea lions, condylarths. It was pretty boring shooting up mesquite bushes, so we hunkered down behind some rocks, Father and I, he hunkered down behind his rocks and I hunkered down behind my rocks, and we commenced to shooting at each other. That was interesting.

•

My father is looking at himself in a mirror. He is wearing a large hat (straw) on which there are a number of blue and yellow plastic jonquils. He says: "How do I look?"

•

Lars Bang took the sack from me and without asking permission reached inside, withdrawing one of the straw-wrapped bottles of claret. "Here's something!" he exclaimed, reading the label. "A gift for the master, I don't doubt!" Then, regarding me steadily all the while, he took up an awl and lifted the cork. There were two other men seated at the pantry table, dressed in the blue-and-green livery, and with them a dark-haired, beautiful girl, quite young, who said nothing and looked at no one. Lars Bang obtained glasses, kicked a chair in my direction, and poured drinks all round. "To your health!" he said (with what I thought an ironical overtone) and we drank. "This young man," Lars Bang said, nodding at me, "is here seeking our advice on a very complicated business. A murder, I believe you said?" "I said nothing of the kind. I seek information about an accident." The claret was soon exhausted. Without looking at me, Lars Bang opened a second bottle and set it in the center of the table. The beautiful dark-haired girl ignored me along with all the others. For my part, I felt I had conducted myself rather well thus far. I had not protested when the wine was made free of (after all, they would be accustomed to levying a sort of tax on anything entering through the back door). But also I had not permitted his word "murder" to be used, but instead specified the use of the word "accident." Therefore I was, in general, comfortable sitting at the table drinking the wine, for which I have no better head than had my father. "Well," said Lars Bang, at length, "I will relate the circumstances of the accident, and you may judge for yourself as to whether myself and my master, the Lensgreve Aklefeldt, were at fault." I absorbed this news with a slight shock. A count! I had selected a man of very high rank indeed to put my question to. In a moment my accumulated self-confidence drained away. A count! Mother of God, have mercy on me.

•

There is my father, peering through an open door into an empty house. He is accompanied by a dog (small dog; not the same dog as before). He looks into the empty room. He says: "Anybody home?"

•

There is my father, sitting in his bed, weeping.

•

"It was a Friday," Lars Bang began, as if he were telling a tavern story. "The hour was close upon noon and my master directed me to drive him to King's New Square, where he had some business. We were proceeding there at a modest easy pace, for he was in no great hurry. Judge of my astonishment when, passing through the drapers' quarter, we found ourselves set upon by an elderly man, thoroughly drunk, who flung himself at my lead pair and began cutting at their legs with a switch, in the most vicious manner imaginable. The poor dumb brutes reared, of course, in fright and fear, for," Lars Bang said piously, "they are accustomed to the best of care, and never a blow do they receive from me, or from the other coachman, Rik, for the count is especially severe upon this point, that his animals be well-treated. The horses, then, were rearing and plunging; it was all I could do to hold them; I shouted at the man, who fell back for an instant. The count stuck his head out of the window, to inquire as to the nature of the trouble; and I told him that a drunken man had attacked our horses. Your father, in his blindness, being not content with the mischief he had already worked, ran back in again, close to the animals, and began madly cutting at their legs with his stick. At this renewed attack the horses, frightened out of their wits, jerked the reins from my hands, and ran headlong over your father, who fell beneath their hooves. The heavy wheels of the carriage passed over him (I felt two quite distinct thumps), his body caught upon a projection under the boot, and he was dragged some forty feet, over the cobblestones. I was attempting, with all my might, merely to hang on to the box, for, having taken the bit between their teeth, the horses were in no mood to tarry; nor could any human agency have stopped them. We flew down the street . . ."

•

My father is attending a class in good behavior.

"Do the men rise when friends greet us while we are sitting in a booth?"

"The men do not rise when they are seated in a booth," he answers, "although they may half-rise and make apologies for not fully rising."

•

". . . the horses turning into the way that leads to King's New Square; and it was not until we reached that place that they stopped and allowed me to quiet them. I wanted to go back and see what had become of the madman, your father, who had attacked us; but my master, vastly angry and shaken up, forbade it. I have never seen him in so fearful a temper as that day; if your father had survived, and my master got his hands on him, it would have gone ill with your father, that's a certainty. And so, you are now in possession of all the facts. I trust you are satisfied, and will drink another bottle of this quite fair claret you have brought us, and be on your way." Before I had time to frame a reply, the dark-haired girl spoke. "Bang is an absolute bloody liar," she said.

•

Etc.

Paraguay

The upper part of the plain that we had crossed the day before was now white with snow, and it was evident that there was a storm raging behind us and that we had only just crossed the Burji La in time to escape it. We camped in a slight hollow at Sekbachan, eighteen miles from Malik Mar, the night as still as the previous one and the temperature the same; it seemed as if the Deosai Plains were not going to be so formidable as they had been described; but the third day a storm of hail, sleet, and snow alternately came at noon when we began to ascend the Sari Sangar Pass, 14,200 feet, and continued with only a few minutes' intermission till four o'clock. The top of the pass is a fairly level valley containing two lakes, their shores formed of boulders that seemed impossible to ride over. The men slid and stumbled so much that I would not let anyone lead my pony for fear of pulling him over; he was old and slow but perfectly splendid here, picking his way among the rocks without a falter. At the summit there is a cairn on which each man threw a stone, and here it is customary to give payment to the coolies. I paid each man his agreed-upon wage, and, alone, began the descent. Ahead was Paraguay.[1]

Where Paraguay Is

Thus I found myself in a strange country. This Paraguay is not the Paraguay that exists on our maps. It is not to be found on the continent, South America; it is not a political subdivision of that continent, with a population of 2,161,000 and a capital city named Asunción. This Paraguay exists elsewhere. Now, moving toward the first of the "silver cities," I was tired but also elated and alert. Flights of white meat moved through the sky overhead in the direction of the dim piles of buildings.

Jean Mueller

Entering the city I was approached, that first day, by a dark girl wrapped in a red shawl. The edges of the shawl were fringed, and the tip of each strand of fringe was a bob of silver. The girl at once placed her hands on my hips, standing facing me; she smiled, and exerted a slight pull. I was claimed as her guest; her name was Jean Mueller. *"Teníamos grandes deseos de conocerlo,"* she said. I asked how she knew I had arrived and she said, "Everyone knows." We then proceeded to her house, a large, modern structure some distance from the center of the city; there I was shown into a room containing a bed, a desk, a chair, bookcases, a fireplace, a handsome piano in a cherrywood case. I was told that when I had rested I might join her downstairs and might then meet her husband; before leaving the room she sat down before the piano, and, almost mischievously, played a tiny sonata of Bibblemann's.

Temperature

Temperature controls activity to a remarkable degree. By and large, adults here raise their walking speed and show more spontaneous movement as the temperature rises. But the temperature-dependent pattern of activity is complex. For instance, the males move twice as fast at 60 degrees as they do at 35 degrees, but above 60 degrees speed decreases. The females show more complicated behavior; they increase spontaneous activity as the temperature rises from 40 to 48 degrees, become less active between 49 and 66 degrees, and above 66 degrees again go into a rising tempo of spontaneous movements up to the lethal temperature of 77 degrees. Temperature also (here as elsewhere) plays a critical role in the reproductive process. In the so-called "silver cities" there is a particular scale—66, 67, 68, 69 degrees—at which intercourse occurs (and only within that scale). In the "gold" areas, the scale does not, apparently, apply.

Herko Mueller

Herko Mueller walks through gold and silver leaves, awarded, in the summer months, to those who have produced the best pastiche of the emotions. He is smiling because he did not win one of these prizes, which the people of Paraguay seek to avoid. He is tall, brown, wears a funny short beard, and is fond of zippered suits in brilliant colors: yellow, green, violet. He is, professionally, an arbiter of comedy. "A sort of drama critic?" "More what you would term an umpire. The members of the audience are given a set of rules and the rules constitute the comedy. Our comedies seek to reach the imagination. When you are looking at something, you cannot imagine it." In the evenings I have wet sand to walk upon—long stretches of beach with the sea tasting the edges. Getting back into my clothes after a swim, I discover a strange thing: a sand dollar under my shirt. It is strange because this sand is sifted twice daily to remove impurities and maintain whiteness. And the sea itself, the New Sea, is not programmed for echinoderms.

Error

A government error resulting in the death of a statistically insignificant portion of the population (less than one-fortieth of one per cent) has made people uneasy. A skelp of questions and answers is fused at high temperature (1400° C) and then passed through a series of protracted caresses. Amelioration of the condition results. Paraguay is not old. It is new, a new country. Rough sketches suggest its "look." Heavy yellow drops like pancake batter fall from its sky. I hold a bouquet of umbrellas in each hand. A phrase of Herko Mueller's: *"Y un 60% son mestizos: gloria, orgullo, presente y futuro del Paraguay"* (". . . the glory, pride, present and future of Paraguay"). The country's existence is "predictive," he says, and I myself have noticed a sort of frontier ambience. There are problems. The problem of shedding skin. Thin discarded shells like disposable plastic gloves are found in the street.

Rationalization

The problems of art. New artists have been obtained. These do not object to, and indeed argue enthusiastically for, the rationalization process. Production is up. Quality-control devices have been installed at those points where the interests of artists and audience intersect. Shipping and distribution have been improved out of all recognition. (It is in this area, they say in Paraguay, that traditional practices were most blameworthy.) The rationalized art is dispatched from central art dumps to regional art dumps, and from there into the lifestreams of cities. Each citizen is given as much art as his system can tolerate. Marketing considerations have not been allowed to dictate product mix; rather, each artist is encouraged to maintain, in his software, highly personal, even idiosyncratic, standards (the so-called "hand of the artist" concept). Rationalization produces simpler circuits and, therefore, a saving in hardware. Each artist's product is translated into a statement in symbolic logic. The statement is then "minimized" by various clever methods. The simpler statement is translated back into the design of a simpler circuit. Foamed by a number of techniques, the art is then run through heavy steel rollers. Flip-flop switches control its further development. Sheet art is generally dried in smoke and is dark brown in color. Bulk art is air-dried, and changes color in particular historical epochs.

Skin

Ignoring a letter from the translator Jean sat on a rubber pad doing exercises designed to loosen the skin. Scores of diamond-shaped lights abraded her arms and legs. The light placed a pattern of false information in those zones most susceptible to tearing. Whistling noises accompanied the lights. The process of removing the leg skin is private. Tenseness is eased by the application of a cream, heavy yellow drops like pancake batter. I held several umbrellas over her legs. A man across the street pretending not to watch us. Then the skin placed in the green official receptacles.

The Wall

Our design for the lift tower left us with a vast blind wall of *in situ* concrete. There was thus the danger of having a dreary expanse of blankness in that immensely important part of the building. A solution had to be found. The great wall space would provide an opportunity for a gesture of thanks to the people of Paraguay; a stone would be placed in front of it, and, instead of standing in the shadows, the Stele of the Measures would be brought there also. The wall would be divided, by means of softly worn paths, into doors. These, varying in size from the very large to the very small, would have different colors and thicknesses. Some would open, some would not, and this would change from week to week, or from hour to hour, or in accord with sounds made by people standing in front of them. Long lines or tracks would run from the doors into the roaring public spaces.[2]

Silence

In the larger stores silence (damping materials) is sold in paper sacks like cement. Similarly, the softening of language usually lamented as a falling off from former practice is in fact a clear response to the proliferation of surfaces and stimuli. Imprecise sentences lessen the strain of close tolerances. Silence is also available in the form of white noise. The extension of white noise to the home by means of leased wire from a central generating point has been useful, Herko says. The analogous establishment of "white space" in a system paralleling the existing park system has also been beneficial. Anechoic chambers placed randomly about the city (on the model of telephone booths) are said to have actually saved lives. Wood is becoming rare. They are now paying for yellow pine what was formerly paid for rosewood. Relational methods govern the layout of cities. Curiously, in some of the most successful projects the design has been swung upon small collections of rare animals spaced (on the lost-horse principle) on a lack of grid. Carefully calculated mixes: mambas, the black wrasse, the giselle. Electrolytic jelly exhibiting a capture ratio far in excess of standard is used to fix the animals in place.

Terror

We rushed down to the ends of the waves, apertures through which threatening lines might be seen. Arbiters registered serial numbers of the (complex of threats) with ticks on a great, brown board. Jean meanwhile, unaffected, was casting about on the beach for driftwood, brown washed pieces of wood laced with hundreds of tiny hairline cracks. Such is the smoothness of surfaces in Paraguay that anything not smooth is valuable. She explains to me that in demanding (and receiving) explanations you are once more brought to a stop. You have got, really, no farther than you were before. "Therefore we try to keep everything open, go forward avoiding the final explanation. If we inadvertently receive it, we are instructed to 1) pretend that it is just another error, or 2) misunderstand it. Creative misunderstanding is crucial." Creation of new categories of anxiety which must be bandaged or "patched." The expression "put a patch on it." There are "hot" and "cold" patches and specialists in the application of each. Rhathymia is the preferred mode of presentation of the self.

The Temple

Turning sharply to the left I came upon, in a grove of trees, a temple of some sort, abandoned, littered with empty boxes, the floor coated with a thin layer of lime. I prayed. Then drawing out my flask I refreshed myself with apple juice. Everyone in Paraguay has the same fingerprints. There are crimes but people chosen at random are punished for them. Everyone is liable for everything. An extension of the principle, there but for the grace of God go I. Sexual life is very free. There are rules but these are like the rules of chess, intended to complicate and enrich the game. I made love to Jean Mueller while her husband watched. There have been certain technical refinements. The procedures we use (called here "impalement") are used in Paraguay but also new techniques I had never before encountered, "dimidiation" and "quartering." These I found very refreshing.

Microminiaturization

Microminiaturization leaves enormous spaces to be filled. Disposability of the physical surround has psychological consequences. The example of the child's anxiety occasioned by the family's move to a new home may be cited. Everything physical in Paraguay is getting smaller and smaller. Walls thin as a thought, locomotive-substitutes no bigger than ball-point pens. Paraguay, then, has big empty spaces in which men wander, trying to touch something. Preoccupation with skin (on and off, wrinkling, the new skin, pink fresh, taut) possibly a response to this. Stories about skin, histories of particular skins. But no jokes! Some 700,000 photographs of nuclear events were lost when the great library of Paraguay burned. Particle identification was set back many years. Rather than recreate the former physics, a new physics based on the golden section (proliferation of golden sections) was constructed. As a system of explanation almost certain to be incorrect it enjoys enormous prestige here.

Behind the Wall

Behind the wall there is a field of red snow. I had expected that to enter it would be forbidden, but Jean said no, walk about in it, as much as you like. I had expected that walking in it one would leave no footprints, or that there would be some other anomaly of that kind, but there were no anomalies; I left footprints and felt the cold of red snow underfoot. I said to Jean Mueller, "What is the point of this red snow?" "The intention of the red snow, the reason it is isolated behind the wall, yet not forbidden, is its soft glow—as if it were lighted from beneath. You must have noticed it; you've been standing here for twenty minutes." "But what does it do?" "Like any other snow, it invites contemplation and walking about in." The snow rearranged itself into a smooth, red surface without footprints. It had a red glow, as if lighted from beneath. It seemed to proclaim itself a mystery, but one there was no point in solving—an ongoing low-grade mystery.

Departure

Then I was shown the plan, which is kept in a box. Herko Mueller opened the box with a key (everyone has a key). "Here is the plan," he said. "It governs more or less everything. It is a way of allowing a very wide range of tendencies to interact." The plan was a number of analyses of Brownian motion equipped, at each end, with alligator clips. Then the bell rang and the space became crowded, hundreds of men and women standing there waiting for the marshals to establish some sort of order. I had been chosen, Herko said, to head the column (on the principle of the least-likely-leader). We robed; I folded my arms around the mace. We began the descent (into? out of?) Paraguay.

1. Quoted from *A Summer Ride Through Western Tibet,* by Jane E. Duncan, Collins, London, 1906. Slightly altered.
2. Quoted from *The Modular,* by Le Corbusier, M.I.T. Press, Cambridge, 1954. Slightly altered.

The Falling Dog

Yes, a dog jumped on me out of a high window. I think it was the third floor, or the fourth floor. Or the third floor. Well, it knocked me down. I had my chin on the concrete. Well, he didn't bark before he jumped. It was a silent dog. I was stretched out on the concrete with the dog on my back. The dog was looking at me, his muzzle curled round my ear, his breath was bad, I said "Get off."

He did. He walked away looking back over his shoulder. "Christ," I said. Crumbs of concrete had been driven into my chin. "For God's sake," I said. The dog was four or five metres down the sidewalk, standing still. Looking back at me over his shoulder.

gay dogs falling
sense in which you would say of a thing,
it's a dog, as you would say, it's a lemon

rain of dogs like rain of frogs
or shower of objects dropped to confuse enemy radar

Well, it was a standoff. I was on the concrete. He was standing there. Neither of us spoke. I wondered what he was like (the dog's life). I was curious about the dog. Then I understood why I was curious.

wrapped or bandaged. vulnerability but also
aluminum
plexiglas
anti-hairy materials
vaudeville (the slide for life)

(Of course I instantly made up a scenario to explain everything. Involving a mysterious ((very beautiful)) woman. Her name is Sophie. I follow the dog to her house. "The dog brought me." There is a ringing sound. "What is that ringing?" "That is the electric eye." "Did I break a beam?" "You and the dog together. The dog is only admitted if he brings someone." "What is that window he jumped out of?" "That is his place." "But he comes here because . . ." "His food is here." Sophie smiles and puts a hand on my arm. "Now you must go." "Take the dog back to his place and then come back here?" "No, just take the dog back to his place. That will be enough. When he has finished eating." "Is that all there is to it?" "I needed the beam broken," Sophie says with a piteous look ((Sax Rohmer)). "When the beam is broken, the bell rings. The bell summons a man." "Another man." "Yes. A Swiss." "I could do whatever it is he does." "No. You are for breaking the beam and taking the dog back to his place." I hear him then, the Swiss. I hear his motorcycle. The door opens, he enters, a real brute, muscled, lots of fur ((Olympia Press)). "Why is the dog still here?" "This man refuses to take him back." The Swiss grabs the dog under the muzzle mock playfully. "He wants to stay!" the Swiss says, to the dog. *"He wants to stay!"* Then the Swiss turns to me. "You're not going to take the dog back?" Threatening look, gestures, etc., etc. "No," I say. "The dog jumped on my back, out of a window. A very high window, the third floor or the fourth floor. My chin was driven into the concrete." "What do I care about your flaming chin? I don't think you understand your function. Your function is to get knocked down by the dog, follow the dog here and break the beam, then take the dog back to his place. There's no reason in the world why we should stand here and listen to a lot of flaming nonsense about your flaming etc. etc. . . .")

I looked at the dog. He looked at me.

who else has done dogs?
Baskin, Bacon, Landseer, Hogarth, Hals

with leashes trailing as they fall

with dog impedimenta following:
bowl, bone, collar, license, Gro-pup

I noticed that he was an Irish setter, rust-colored. He noticed that I was a Welsh sculptor, buff-colored (no, really, what did he notice? how does he think?). I reflected that he was probably a nice dog from a good home (bourgeois dog) but with certain unfortunate habits like jumping on people from high windows (rationalization: he is a member of the television generation and thus—)

Well, I read a letter, then. A letter that had come to me from Germany, that had been in my pocket. I hadn't wanted to read it before but now I read it. It seemed a good time.

Mr. XXXX XXXXXXXX
c/o Blue Gallery
Madison and Eighty-first St.
New York, N.Y.

Dear Mr. XXXXXXXX:

For the above-mentioned publishers I am preparing a book of recent American sculptors. This work shall not become a collection of gee-gaws and so, it tries to be an aimed presentation of the qualitative best recent American sculptors. I personally am fascinated from your collected YAWNING MAN series of sculptors as well as the YAWNING lithographs. For this reason I absolutely want to include a new figure or figures from you if there are new ones. The critiques of your first show in Basel had been very bad. The German reviewers are coming from such immemorial conceptions of art that they did not know what to do with your sculptors. And I wish a better welcome to your contribution to this book when it is published here. Please send recent photographs of the work plus explanatory text on the YAWNING MAN.

Many thanks! and kindest regards!

Yours,
R. Rondorfer

Well, I was right in not wanting to read that letter. It was kind of this man to be interested in something I was no longer interested in. How was he to know that I was in that unhappiest of states, between images?

But now something new had happened to me.

dogs as a luxury (what do we need them for?)
hounds of heaven

fallen in the sense of fallen angels
flayed dogs falling? musculature
sans skeleton?

But it is well to be suspicious. Sometimes an image is not an image at all but merely an idea. People have wasted years.

I wanted the dog's face. Whereas my old image, the Yawning Man, had been faceless (except for a gap where the mouth was, the yawn itself), I wanted the dog's face. I wanted his expression, falling. I thought of the alternatives: screaming, smiling. And things in between.

dirty and clean dogs
ultra-clean dogs, laboratory animals
thrown or flung dogs
in series, Indian file

an exploded view of the Falling Dog:
head, heart, liver, lights

to the dogs
putting on the dog:
I am telling him something which isn't true

and we are both falling

dog tags!
but forget puns. Cloth falling dogs, the
gingham dog and the etc., etc. Pieces
of cloth dogs falling. Or quarter-inch
plywood in layers, the layers separated
by an inch or two of airspace. Like old
triple-wing aircraft

dog-ear (pages falling with corners bent back)

Tray: cafeteria trays of some obnoxious brown plastic
But enough puns

Group of tiny hummingbird-sized falling dogs
Massed in upper corners of a room with high ceilings, 14–17 foot
in rows, in ranks, on their backs

Well, I understood then that this was my new image, The Falling Dog. My old image, the Yawning Man, was played out. I had done upward of two thousand Yawning Men in every known material, and I was tired of it. Images fray, tatter, empty themselves. I had seven good years with that image, the Yawning Man, but—

But now I had the Falling Dog, what happiness.

(flights? sheets?)
of falling dogs, flat falling dogs like sails
Day-Glo dogs falling

am I being sufficiently skeptical?
try it out

die like a
dog-eat-dog
proud as a dog in shoes
dogfight
doggerel
dogmatic

am I being over-impressed by the circumstances
suddenness
pain
but it's a gift. thank you

love me love my

styrofoam?

Well, I got up and brushed off my chin, then. The silent dog was still standing there. I went up to him carefully. He did not move. I had to wonder about what it meant, the Falling Dog, but I didn't have to wonder about it now, I could wonder later. I wrapped my arms around his belly and together we rushed to the studio.

At the Tolstoy Museum

At the Tolstoy Museum we sat and wept. Paper streamers came out of our eyes. Our gaze drifted toward the pictures. They were placed too high on the wall. We suggested to the director that they be lowered six inches at least. He looked unhappy but said he would see to it. The holdings of the Tolstoy Museum consist principally of some thirty thousand pictures of Count Leo Tolstoy.

After they had lowered the pictures we went back to the Tolstoy Museum. I don't think you can peer into one man's face too long—for too long a period. A great many human passions could be discerned, behind the skin.

Tolstoy means "fat" in Russian. His grandfather sent his linen to Holland to be washed. His mother *did not know* any bad words. As a youth he shaved off his eyebrows, hoping they would grow back bushier. He first contracted gonorrhea in 1847. He was once bitten on the face by a bear. He became a vegetarian in 1885. To make himself interesting, he occasionally bowed backward.

Tolstoy's coat

Tolstoy as a youth

I was eating a sandwich at the Tolstoy Museum. The Tolstoy Museum is made of stone—many stones, cunningly wrought. Viewed from the street, it has the aspect of three stacked boxes: the first, second, and third levels. These are of increasing size. The first level is, say, the size of a shoebox, the second level the size of a case of whiskey, and the third level the size of a box that contained a new overcoat. The amazing cantilever of the third level has been much talked about. The glass floor there allows one to look straight down and provides a "floating" feeling. The entire building, viewed from the street, suggests that it is about to fall on you. This the architects relate to Tolstoy's moral authority.

In the basement of the Tolstoy Museum carpenters uncrated new pictures of Count Leo Tolstoy. The huge crates stencilled FRAGILE in red ink . . .

The guards at the Tolstoy Museum carry buckets in which there are stacks of clean white pocket handkerchiefs. More than any other Museum, the Tolstoy Museum induces weeping. Even the bare title of a Tolstoy work, with its burden of love, can induce weeping—for example, the article titled "Who Should Teach Whom to Write, We the Peasant Children or the Peasant Children Us?" Many people stand before this article, weeping. Too, those who are caught by Tolstoy's eyes, in the various portraits, room after room after room, are not unaffected by the experience. It is like, people say, committing a small crime and being discovered at it by your father, who stands in four doorways, looking at you.

At Starogladkovskaya,
about 1852

Tiger hunt, Siberia

I was reading a story of Tolstoy's at the Tolstoy Museum. In this story a bishop is sailing on a ship. One of his fellow-passengers tells the bishop about an island on which three hermits live. The hermits are said to be extremely devout. The bishop is seized with a desire to see and talk with the hermits. He persuades the captain of the ship to anchor near the island. He goes ashore in a small boat. He speaks to the hermits. The hermits tell the bishop how they worship God. They have a prayer that goes: "Three of You, three of us, have mercy on us." The bishop feels that this is a prayer prayed in the wrong way. He undertakes to teach the hermits the Lord's Prayer. The hermits learn the Lord's Prayer but with the greatest difficulty. Night has fallen by the time they have got it correctly.

The bishop returns to his ship, happy that he has been able to assist the hermits in their worship. The ship sails on. The bishop sits alone on deck, thinking about the experiences of the day. He sees a light in the sky, behind the ship. The light is cast by the three hermits floating over the water, hand in hand, without moving their feet. They catch up with the ship, saying: "We have forgotten, servant of God, we have forgotten your teaching!" They ask him to teach them again. The bishop crosses himself. Then he tells the hermits that their prayer, too, reaches God. "It is not for me to teach you. Pray for us sinners!" The bishop bows to the deck. The hermits fly back over the sea, hand in hand, to their island.

The story is written in a very simple style. It is said to originate in a folk tale. There is a version of it in St. Augustine. I was incredibly depressed by reading this story. Its beauty. Distance.

The Anna-Vronsky Pavilion

At the Tolstoy Museum, sadness grasped the 741 Sunday visitors. The Museum was offering a series of lectures on the text "Why Do Men Stupefy Themselves?" The visitors were made sad by these eloquent speakers, who were probably right.

People stared at tiny pictures of Turgenev, Nekrasov, and Fet. These and other small pictures hung alongside extremely large pictures of Count Leo Tolstoy.

In the plaza, a sinister musician played a wood trumpet while two children watched.

We considered the 640,086 pages (Jubilee Edition) of the author's published work. Some people wanted him to go away, but other people were glad we had him. "He has been a lifelong source of inspiration to me," one said.

I haven't made up my mind. Standing here in the "Summer in the Country" Room, several hazes passed over my eyes. Still, I think I will march on to "A Landlord's Morning." Perhaps something vivifying will happen to me there.

At the disaster (arrow indicates Tolstoy)

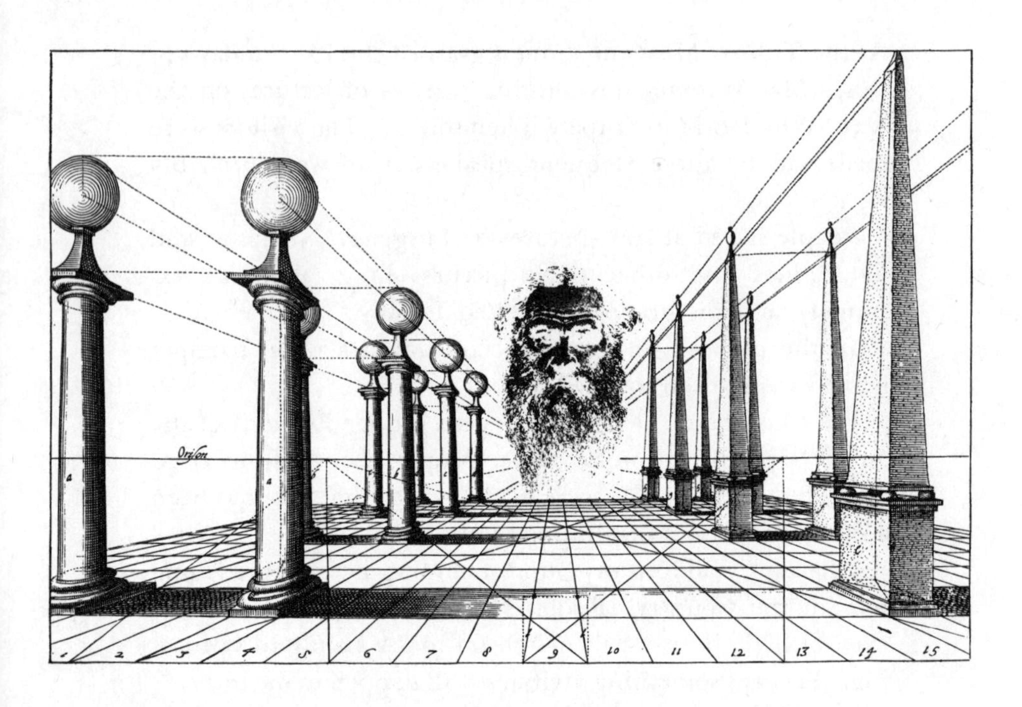

Museum plaza with monumental head (Closed Mondays)

The Policemen's Ball

Horace, a policeman, was making Rock Cornish Game Hens for a special supper. The Game Hens are frozen solid, Horace thought. He was wearing his blue uniform pants.

Inside the Game Hens were the giblets in a plastic bag. Using his needlenose pliers Horace extracted the frozen giblets from the interior of the birds. Tonight is the night of the Policemen's Ball, Horace thought. We will dance the night away. But first, these Game Hens must go into a three-hundred-and-fifty-degree oven.

Horace shined his black dress shoes. Would Margot "put out" tonight? On this night of nights? Well, if she didn't—Horace regarded the necks of the birds which had been torn asunder by the pliers. No, he reflected, that is not a proper thought. Because I am a member of the force. I must try to keep my hatred under control. I must try to be an example for the rest of the people. Because if they can't trust us . . . the blue men . . .

In the dark, outside the Policemen's Ball, the horrors waited for Horace and Margot.

Margot was alone. Her roommates were in Provincetown for the weekend. She put pearl-colored lacquer on her nails to match the pearl of her new-bought gown. Police colonels and generals will be there, she thought. The Pendragon of Police himself. Whirling past the dais, I will glance upward. The pearl of my eyes meeting the steel gray of high rank.

Margot got into a cab and went over to Horace's place. The cabdriver was thinking: A nice-looking piece. I could love her.

Horace removed the birds from the oven. He slipped little gold frills, which had been included in the package, over the ends of the drumsticks. Then he uncorked the wine, thinking: This is a town without pity, this town. For those whose voices lack the crack of authority. Luckily the uniform . . . Why won't she surrender her person? Does she think she can resist the force? The force of the force?

"These birds are delicious."

Driving Horace and Margot smoothly to the Armory, the new cabdriver thought about basketball.

Why do they always applaud the man who makes the shot?
Why don't they applaud the ball?
It is the ball that actually goes into the net.
The man doesn't go into the net.
Never have I seen a man going into the net.

Twenty thousand policemen of all grades attended the annual fete. The scene was Camelot, with gay colors and burgees. The interior of the Armory had been roofed with lavish tenting. Police colonels and generals looked down on the dark uniforms, white gloves, silvery ball gowns.

"Tonight?"

"Horace, not now. This scene is so brilliant. I want to remember it."

Horace thought: It? Not me?

The Pendragon spoke. "I ask you to be reasonable with the citizens. They pay our salaries after all. I know that they are difficult sometimes, obtuse sometimes, even criminal sometimes, as we often run across in our line of work. But I ask you despite all to be reasonable. I know it is hard. I know it is not easy. I know that for instance when you see a big car, a '70 Biscayne hardtop, cutting around a corner at a pretty fair clip, with three in the front and three in the back, and they are all mixed up, ages and sexes and colors, your natural impulse is to— I know your first thought is, All those people! Together! And your second thought is, Force! But I must ask you in the name of force itself to be restrained. For force, that great principle, is most honored in the breach and the observance. And that is where you men are, in the breach. You are fine men, the finest. You are Americans. So for the sake of America, be careful. Be reasonable. Be slow. In the name of the Father and of the Son and of the Holy Ghost. And now I would like to introduce Vercingetorix, leader of the firemen, who brings us a few words of congratulation from that fine body of men."

Waves of applause for the Pendragon filled the tented area.

"He is a handsome older man," Margot said.

"He was born in a Western state and advanced to his present position through raw merit," Horace told her.

The government of Czechoslovakia sent observers to the Policemen's Ball. "Our police are not enough happy," Colonel-General Čepicky explained. "We seek ways to improve them. This is a way. It may not be the best way of all possible ways, but . . . Also I like to drink the official whiskey! It makes me gay!"

A bartender thought: Who is that yellow-haired girl in the pearl costume? She is stacked.

The mood of the Ball changed. The dancing was more serious now. Margot's eyes sparkled from the jorums of champagne she had drunk. She felt Horace's delicately Game Hen-flavored breath on her cheek. I will give him what he wants, she decided. Tonight. His heroism deserves it. He stands between us and them. He represents what is best in the society: decency, order, safety, strength, sirens, smoke. No, he does not represent smoke. Firemen represent smoke. Great billowing oily black clouds. That Vercingetorix has a noble look. With whom is Vercingetorix dancing, at present?

The horrors waited outside patiently. Even policemen, the horrors thought. We get even policemen, in the end.

In Horace's apartment, a gold frill was placed on a pearl toe.

The horrors had moved outside Horace's apartment. Not even policemen and their ladies are safe, the horrors thought. No one is safe. Safety does not exist. Ha ha ha ha ha ha ha ha ha ha!

The Glass Mountain

1. I was trying to climb the glass mountain.
2. The glass mountain stands at the corner of Thirteenth Street and Eighth Avenue.
3. I had attained the lower slope.
4. People were looking up at me.
5. I was new in the neighborhood.
6. Nevertheless I had acquaintances.
7. I had strapped climbing irons to my feet and each hand grasped a sturdy plumber's friend.
8. I was 200 feet up.
9. The wind was bitter.
10. My acquaintances had gathered at the bottom of the mountain to offer encouragement.
11. "Shithead."
12. "Asshole."
13. Everyone in the city knows about the glass mountain.

14. People who live here tell stories about it.
15. It is pointed out to visitors.
16. Touching the side of the mountain, one feels coolness.
17. Peering into the mountain, one sees sparkling blue-white depths.
18. The mountain towers over that part of Eighth Avenue like some splendid, immense office building.
19. The top of the mountain vanishes into the clouds, or on cloudless days, into the sun.
20. I unstuck the righthand plumber's friend leaving the lefthand one in place.
21. Then I stretched out and reattached the righthand one a little higher up, after which I inched my legs into new positions.
22. The gain was minimal, not an arm's length.
23. My acquaintances continued to comment.
24. "Dumb motherfucker."
25. I was new in the neighborhood.
26. In the streets were many people with disturbed eyes.
27. Look for yourself.
28. In the streets were hundreds of young people shooting up in doorways, behind parked cars.
29. Older people walked dogs.
30. The sidewalks were full of dogshit in brilliant colors: ocher, umber, Mars yellow, sienna, viridian, ivory black, rose madder.
31. And someone had been apprehended cutting down trees, a row of elms broken-backed among the VWs and Valiants.
32. Done with a power saw, beyond a doubt.
33. I was new in the neighborhood yet I had accumulated acquaintances.

34. My acquaintances passed a brown bottle from hand to hand.
35. "Better than a kick in the crotch."
36. "Better than a poke in the eye with a sharp stick."
37. "Better than a slap in the belly with a wet fish."
38. "Better than a thump on the back with a stone."
39. "Won't he make a splash when he falls, now?"
40. "I hope to be here to see it. Dip my handkerchief in the blood."
41. "Fart-faced fool."
42. I unstuck the lefthand plumber's friend leaving the righthand one in place.
43. And reached out.
44. To climb the glass mountain, one first requires a good reason.
45. No one has ever climbed the mountain on behalf of science, or in search of celebrity, or because the mountain was a challenge.
46. Those are not good reasons.
47. But good reasons exist.
48. At the top of the mountain there is a castle of pure gold, and in a room in the castle tower sits . . .
49. My acquaintances were shouting at me.
50. "Ten bucks you bust your ass in the next four minutes!"
51. . . . a beautiful enchanted symbol.
52. I unstuck the righthand plumber's friend leaving the lefthand one in place.
53. And reached out.
54. It was cold there at 206 feet and when I looked down I was not encouraged.
55. A heap of corpses both of horses and riders ringed the

69. My acquaintances were prising out the gold teeth of not-yet-dead knights.
70. In the streets were people concealing their calm behind a façade of vague dread.
71. "The conventional symbol (such as the nightingale, often associated with melancholy), even though it is recognized only through agreement, is not a sign (like the traffic light) because, again, it presumably arouses deep feelings and is regarded as possessing properties beyond what the eye alone sees." (*A Dictionary of Literary Terms*)
72. A number of nightingales with traffic lights tied to their legs flew past me.
73. A knight in pale pink armor appeared above me.
74. He sank, his armor making tiny shrieking sounds against the glass.
75. He gave me a sideways glance as he passed me.
76. He uttered the word "*Muerte*" as he passed me.
77. I unstuck the righthand plumber's friend.
78. My acquaintances were debating the question, which of them would get my apartment?
79. I reviewed the conventional means of attaining the castle.
80. The conventional means of attaining the castle are as follows: "The eagle dug its sharp claws into the tender flesh of the youth, but he bore the pain without a sound, and seized the bird's two feet with his hands. The creature in terror lifted him high up into the air and began to circle the castle. The youth held on bravely. He saw the glittering palace, which by the pale rays of the moon looked like a dim lamp; and he saw the windows and balconies of the castle tower. Drawing a small knife from his belt, he cut off both the eagle's feet. The bird rose up in the air with a yelp, and the youth dropped lightly onto a broad

balcony. At the same moment a door opened, and he saw a courtyard filled with flowers and trees, and there, the beautiful enchanted princess." (*The Yellow Fairy Book*)

81. I was afraid.
82. I had forgotten the Bandaids.
83. When the eagle dug its sharp claws into my tender flesh—
84. Should I go back for the Bandaids?
85. But if I went back for the Bandaids I would have to endure the contempt of my acquaintances.
86. I resolved to proceed without the Bandaids.
87. "In some centuries, his [man's] imagination has made life an intense practice of all the lovelier energies." (John Masefield)
88. The eagle dug its sharp claws into my tender flesh.
89. But I bore the pain without a sound, and seized the bird's two feet with my hands.
90. The plumber's friends remained in place, standing at right angles to the side of the mountain.
91. The creature in terror lifted me high in the air and began to circle the castle.
92. I held on bravely.
93. I saw the glittering palace, which by the pale rays of the moon looked like a dim lamp; and I saw the windows and balconies of the castle tower.
94. Drawing a small knife from my belt, I cut off both the eagle's feet.
95. The bird rose up in the air with a yelp, and I dropped lightly onto a broad balcony.
96. At the same moment a door opened, and I saw a courtyard filled with flowers and trees, and there, the beautiful enchanted symbol.
97. I approached the symbol, with its layers of meaning,

but when I touched it, it changed into only a beautiful princess.

98. I threw the beautiful princess headfirst down the mountain to my acquaintances.
99. Who could be relied upon to deal with her.
100. Nor are eagles plausible, not at all, not for a moment.

The Explanation

Q: Do you believe that this machine could be helpful in changing the government?

A: Changing the government . . .

Q: Making it more responsive to the needs of the people?

A: I don't know what it is. What does it do?

Q: Well, look at it.

A: It offers no clues.

Q: It has a certain . . . reticence.

A: I don't know what it does.

Q: A lack of confidence in the machine?

Q: Is the novel dead?

A: Oh yes. Very much so.

Q: What replaces it?

A: I should think that it is replaced by what existed before it was invented.

Q: The same thing?

A: The same sort of thing.

Q: Is the bicycle dead?

Q: You don't trust the machine?

A: Why should I trust it?

Q: (States his own lack of interest in machines)

Q: What a beautiful sweater.

A: Thank you. I don't want to worry about machines.

Q: What do you worry about?

A: I was standing on the corner waiting for the light to change when I noticed, across the street among the people there waiting for the light to change, an extraordinarily handsome girl who was looking at me. Our eyes met, I looked away, then I looked again, she was looking away, the light changed. I moved into the street as did she. First I looked at her again to see if she was still looking at me, she wasn't but I was aware that she was aware of me. I decided to smile. I smiled but in a curious way—the smile was supposed to convey that I was interested in her but also that I was aware that the situation was funny. But I bungled it. I smirked. I dislike even the word "smirk." There was, you know, the moment when we passed each other. I had resolved to look at her directly in that moment. I tried but she was looking a bit to the left of me, she was looking fourteen inches to the left of my eyes.

Q: This is the sort of thing that—

A: I want to go back and do it again.

Q: Now that you've studied it for a bit, can you explain how it works?

A: Of course. (Explanation)

Q: Is she still removing her blouse?

A: Yes, still.

Q: Do you want to have your picture taken with me?

A: I don't like to have my picture taken.

Q: Do you believe that, at some point in the future, one will be able to achieve sexual satisfaction, "complete" sexual satisfaction, for instance by taking a pill?

A: I doubt that it's impossible.

Q: You don't like the idea.

A: No. I think that under those conditions, we would know less than we do now.

Q: Know less about each other.

A: Of course.

Q: It has beauties.

A: The machine.

Q: Yes. We construct these machines not because we confidently expect them to do what they are designed to do—change the government in this instance—but because we intuit a machine, out there, glowing like a shopping center. . . .

A: You have to contend with a history of success.

Q: Which has gotten us nowhere.

A: (Extends consolation)

Q: What did you do then?

A: I walked on a tree. For twenty steps.

Q: What sort of tree?

A: A dead tree. I can't tell one from another. It may have been an oak. I was reading a book.

Q: What was the book?

A: I don't know, I can't tell one from another. They're not like films. With films you can remember, at a minimum, who the actors were. . . .

Q: What was she doing?

A: Removing her blouse. Eating an apple.

Q: The tree must have been quite large.

A: The tree must have been quite large.

Q: Where was this?

A: Near the sea. I had rope-soled shoes.

Q: I have a number of error messages I'd like to introduce here and I'd like you to study them carefully . . . they're numbered. I'll go over them with you: undefined variable . . . improper sequence of operators . . . improper use of hierarchy . . . missing operator . . . mixed mode, that one's particularly grave . . . argument of a function is fixed-point . . . improper character in constant . . . improper fixed-point constant . . . improper floating-point constant . . . invalid character transmitted in sub-program statement, that's a bitch . . . no END statement.

A: I like them very much.

Q: There are hundreds of others, hundreds and hundreds.

A: You seem emotionless.

Q: That's not true.

A: To what do your emotions . . . adhere, if I can put it that way?

Q: Do you see what she is doing?

A: Removing her blouse.

Q: How does she look?

A: . . . Self-absorbed.

Q: Are you bored with the question-and-answer form?

A: I am bored with it but I realize that it permits many valuable omissions: what kind of day it is, what I'm wearing, what I'm thinking. That's a very considerable advantage, I would say.

Q: I believe in it.

Q: She sang and we listened to her.
A: I was speaking to a tourist.
Q: Their chair is here.
A: I knocked at the door; it was shut.
Q: The soldiers marched toward the castle.
A: I had a watch.
Q: He has struck me.
A: I have struck him.
Q: Their chair is here.
A: We shall not cross the river.
Q: The boats are filled with water.
A: His father will strike him.
Q: Filling his pockets with fruit.

Q: The face . . . the machine has a face. This panel here . . .

A: That one?

Q: Just as the human face developed . . . from fish . . . it's traceable, from, say, the . . . The first mouth was that of a jellyfish. I can't remember the name, the Latin name. . . . But a mouth, there's more to it than just a mouth, a mouth alone is not a face. It went on up through the sharks . . .

A: Up through the sharks . . .

Q: . . . to the snakes. . . .

A: Yes.

Q: The face has *three* main functions, detection of desirable energy sources, direction of the locomotor machinery toward its goal, and capture. . . .

A: Yes.

Q: Capture and preliminary preparation of food. Is this too . . .

A: Not a bit.

Q: The face, a face, also serves as a lure in mate acquisition. The broad, forwardly directed nose—

A: I don't see that on the panel.

Q: Look at it.

A: I don't—

Q: There is an analogy, believe it or not. The . . . We use industrial designers to do the front panels, the controls. Designers, artists. To make the machines attractive to potential buyers. Pure cosmetics. They told us that knife switches were masculine. Men felt . . . So we used a lot of knife switches. . . .

A: I know that a great deal has been written about all this but when I come across such articles, in the magazines or in a newspaper, I don't read them. I'm not interested.

Q: What are your interests?
A: I'm a director of the Schumann Festival.

Q: What is she doing now?
A: Taking off her jeans.
Q: Has she removed her blouse?
A: No, she's still wearing her blouse.
Q: A yellow blouse?
A: Blue.
Q: Well, what is she doing now?
A: Removing her jeans.
Q: What is she wearing underneath?
A: Pants. Panties.
Q: But she's still wearing her blouse?
A: Yes.
Q: Has she removed her panties?
A: Yes.
Q: Still wearing the blouse?
A: Yes. She's walking along a log.
Q: In her blouse. Is she reading a book?
A: No. She has sunglasses.
Q: She's wearing sunglasses?
A: Holding them in her hand.
Q: How does she look?
A: Quite beautiful.

Q: What is the content of Maoism?
A: The content of Maoism is purity.
Q: Is purity quantifiable?
A: Purity has never been quantifiable.
Q: What is the incidence of purity worldwide?
A: Purity occurs in .004 per cent of all cases.
Q: What is purity in the pure state often consonant with?

A: Purity in the pure state is often consonant with madness.

Q: This is not to denigrate madness.

A: This is not to denigrate madness. Madness in the pure state offers an alternative to the reign of right reason.

Q: What is the content of right reason?

A: The content of right reason is rhetoric.

Q: And the content of rhetoric?

A: The content of rhetoric is purity.

Q: Is purity quantifiable?

A: Purity is not quantifiable. It *is* inflatable.

Q: How is our rhetoric preserved against attacks by other rhetorics?

A: Our rhetoric is preserved by our elected representatives. In the fat of their heads.

Q: There's no point in arguing that the machine is wholly successful, but it has its qualities. I don't like to use anthropomorphic language in talking about these machines, but there is one quality . . .

A: What is it?

Q: It's brave.

A: Machines are braver than art.

Q: Since the death of the bicycle.

Q: There are ten rules for operating the machine. The first rule is turn it on.

A: Turn it on.

Q: The second rule is convert the terms. The third rule is rotate the inputs. The fourth rule is you have made a serious mistake.

A: What do I do?

Q: You send the appropriate error message.

A: I will never remember these rules.

Q: I'll repeat them a hundred times.

A: I was happier before.

Q: You imagined it.

A: The issues are not real.

Q: The issues are not real in the sense that they are touchable. The issues raised here are equivalents. Reasons and conclusions exist although they exist elsewhere, not here. Reasons and conclusions are in the air and simple to observe even for those who do not have the leisure to consult or learn to read the publications of the specialized disciplines.

A: The situation bristles with difficulties.

Q: The situation bristles with difficulties but in the end young people and workers will live on the same plane as old people and government officials, for the mutual good of all categories. The phenomenon of masses, in following the law of high numbers, makes possible exceptional and rare events, which—

A: I called her then and told her that I had dreamed about her, that she was naked in the dream, that we were making love. She didn't wish to be dreamed about, she said —not now, not later, not ever, when would I stop. I suggested that it was something over which I had no control. She said that it had all been a long time ago and that she was married to William now, as I knew, and that she didn't want . . . irruptions of this kind. Think of William, she said.

Q: He has struck me.

A: I have struck him.

Q: We have seen them.

A: I was looking at the window.

Q: Their chair is here.

A: She sang and we listened to her.

Q: Soldiers marching toward the castle.
A: I spoke to a tourist.
Q: I knocked at the door.
A: We shall not cross the river.
Q: The river has filled the boats with water.
A: I think that I have seen her with my uncle.
Q: Getting into their motorcar, I heard them.
A: He will strike her if he has lost it.

A (concluding): There's no doubt in my mind that the ballplayers today are the greatest ever. They're brilliant athletes, extremely well coordinated, tremendous in every department. The ballplayers today are so magnificent that scoring is a relatively simple thing for them.

Q: Thank you for confiding in me.

Q: . . . show you a picture of my daughter.

A: Very nice.
Q: I can give you a few references for further reading.
A: (Nose begins to bleed)

Q: What is she doing now?
A: There is a bruise on her thigh. The right.

Kierkegaard Unfair to Schlegel

A: I use the girl on the train a lot. I'm on a train, a European train with compartments. A young girl enters and sits opposite me. She is blond, wearing a short-sleeved sweater, a short skirt. The sweater has white and blue stripes, the skirt is dark blue. The girl has a book, *Introduction to French* or something like that. We are in France but she is not French. She has a book and a pencil. She's extremely self-conscious. She opens the book and begins miming close attention, you know, making marks with the pencil at various points. Meanwhile I am carefully looking out of the window, regarding the terrain. I'm trying to avoid looking at her legs. The skirt has raised itself a bit, you see, there is a lot of leg to look at. I'm also trying to avoid looking at her breasts. They appear to be free under the white-and-blue sweater. There is a small gold pin pinned to the sweater on the left side. It has lettering on it. I can't make out what it says. The girl shifts in her seat, moves from side to side, adjusting her position. She's very very self-aware. All her movements are just a shade overdone. The book is in her lap. Her legs are fairly wide apart, very tanned, the color of—

Q: That's a very common fantasy.
A: All my fantasies are extremely ordinary.
Q: Does it give you pleasure?
A: A poor . . . A rather unsatisfactory . . .
Q: What is the frequency?
A: Oh God who knows. Once in a while. Sometimes.
Q: You're not cooperating.
A: I'm not interested.
Q: I might do an article.
A: I don't like to have my picture taken.
Q: Solipsism plus triumphantism.
A: It's possible.

Q: You're not political?

A: I'm extremely political in a way that does no good to anybody.

Q: You don't participate?

A: I participate. I make demands, sign newspaper advertisements, vote. I make small campaign contributions to the candidate of my choice and turn my irony against the others. But I accomplish nothing. I march, it's ludicrous. In the last march, there were eighty-seven thousand people marching, by the most conservative estimate, and yet being in the midst of them, marching with them . . . I wanted to march with the Stationary Engineers, march under their banner, but two cops prevented me, they said I couldn't enter at that point, I had to go back to the beginning. So I went back to the beginning and marched with the Food Handlers for Peace and Freedom.

Q: What sort of people were they?

A: They looked just like everybody else. It's possible they weren't real food handlers. Maybe just the two holding the sign. I don't know. There were a lot of girls in black pajamas and peasant straw hats, very young girls, high-school girls, running, holding hands in a long chain, laughing. . . .

Q: You've been pretty hard on our machines. You've withheld your enthusiasm, that's damaging . . .

A: I'm sorry.

Q: Do you think your irony could be helpful in changing the government?

A: I think the government is very often in an ironic relation to itself. And that's helpful. For example: we're spending a great deal of money for this army we have, a very large army, beautifully equipped. We're spending something on the order of twenty billions a year for it. Now, the whole point of an army is—what's the word?—deterrence. And the nut of deterrence is credibility. So what does the government do? It goes and sells off its surplus uniforms. And the kids start wearing them, uniforms or parts of uniforms, because they're cheap and have some sort of style. And immediately you get this vast clown army in the streets parodying the real army. And they mix periods, you know, you get parody British grenadiers and parody World War I types and parody Sierra Maestra types. So you have all these kids walking around wearing these filthy uniforms with wound stripes, hash marks, Silver Stars, but also ostrich feathers, Day-Glo vests, amulets containing powdered rhinoceros horn . . . You have this splendid clown army in the streets standing over against the real one. And of course the clown army constitutes a very serious attack on all the ideas which support the real army including the basic notion of having an army at all. The government has opened itself to all this, this undermining of its own credibility, just because it wants to make a few dollars peddling old uniforms. . . .

Q: How is my car?
Q: How is my nail?
Q: How is the taste of my potato?
Q: How is the cook of my potato?
Q: How is my garb?
Q: How is my button?
Q: How is the flower bath?
Q: How is the shame?
Q: How is the plan?
Q: How is the fire?
Q: How is the flue?
Q: How is my mad mother?
Q: How is the aphorism I left with you?

Q: You are an ironist.
A: It's useful.
Q: How is it useful?
A: Well, let me tell you a story. Several years ago I was living in a rented house in Colorado. The house was what is called a rancher—three or four bedrooms, knotty pine or some such on the inside, cedar shakes or something like that on the outside. It was owned by a ski instructor who lived there with his family in the winter. It had what seemed to be hundreds of closets and we immediately discovered that these closets were filled to overflowing with all kinds of play equipment. Never in my life had I seen so much play equip-

ment gathered together in one place outside, say, Abercrombie's. There were bows and arrows and shuffleboard and croquet sets, putting greens and trampolines and things that you strapped to your feet and jumped up and down on, table tennis and jai alai and poker chips and home roulette wheels, chess and checkers and Chinese checkers and balls of all kinds, hoops and nets and wickets, badminton and books and a thousand board games, and a dingus with cymbals on top that you banged on the floor to keep time to the piano. The merest drawer in a bedside table was choked with marked cards and Monopoly money.

Now, suppose I had been of an ironical turn of mind and wanted to make a joke about all this, some sort of joke that would convey that I had noticed the striking degree of boredom implied by the presence of all this impedimenta and one which would also serve to comment upon the particular way of struggling with boredom that these people had chosen. I might have said, for instance, that the remedy is worse than the disease. Or quoted Nietzsche to the effect that the thought of suicide is a great consolation and had helped him through many a bad night. Either of these perfectly good jokes would do to annihilate the situation of being uncomfortable in this house. The shuffleboard sticks, the barbells, balls of all kinds—my joke has, in effect, thrown them out of the world. An amazing magical power!

Now, suppose that I am suddenly curious about this amazing magical power. Suppose I become curious about how my irony actually works—how it functions. I pick up a copy of Kierkegaard's *The Concept of Irony* (the ski instructor is also a student of Kierkegaard) and I am immediately plunged into difficulties. The situation bristles with difficulties. To begin with, Kierkegaard says that the outstanding feature of irony is that it confers upon the ironist a subjective freedom. The subject, the speaker, is negatively free. If what the ironist says is not his meaning, or is the opposite of his meaning, he is free both in relation to others and in relation to himself. He is not bound by what he has said. Irony is a means of depriving the object of its reality in order that the subject may feel free.

Irony deprives the object of its reality when the ironist says something about the object that is not what he means. Kierkegaard distinguishes between the phenomenon (the word) and the essence (the thought or meaning). Truth demands an identity of essence and phenomenon. But with irony quote the phenomenon is not the essence but the opposite of the essence unquote page 264. The object is deprived of its reality by what I have said about it. Regarded in an ironical light, the object shivers, shatters, disappears. Irony is thus destructive and what Kierkegaard worries about a lot is that irony has nothing to put in the place of what it has destroyed. The new actuality—what the ironist has said about the object—is peculiar in that it is a comment upon a former actuality rather than a new actuality. This account of Kierkegaard's account of irony is grossly oversimplified. Now, consider an irony directed not against a given object but against the whole of existence. An irony directed against the whole of existence produces, according to Kierkegaard, estrangement and poetry. The ironist, serially successful in disposing of various objects of his irony, becomes drunk with freedom. He becomes, in Kierkegaard's words, lighter and lighter. Irony becomes an infinite absolute negativity. Quote irony no longer directs itself against this or that particular phenomenon, against a particular thing unquote. Quote the whole of existence has become alien to the ironic subject unquote page 276. For Kierkegaard, the actuality of irony is poetry. This may be clarified by reference to Kierkegaard's treatment of Schlegel.

Schlegel had written a book, a novel, called *Lucinde*. Kierkegaard is very hard on Schlegel and *Lucinde*. Kierkegaard characterizes this novel of Schlegel's as quote poetical unquote page 308. By which he means to suggest that Schlegel has constructed an actuality which is superior to the historical actuality and a substitute for it. By negating the historical actuality poetry quote opens up a higher actuality, expands and transfigures the imperfect into the perfect, and thereby softens and mitigates that deep pain which would darken and obscure all things unquote page 312. That's beautiful. Now this would seem to be a victory for Schlegel, and indeed Kierkegaard says that poetry is a victory over the world. But it is not the case that *Lucinde* is a victory for Schlegel. What is wanted, Kierkegaard says, is not a victory over the world but a reconciliation with the world. And it is soon discovered that although poetry is a kind of reconciliation, the distance between the new actuality, higher and more perfect than the historical actuality, and the historical actuality, lower and more imperfect than the new actuality, produces not a reconciliation but animosity. Quote so that it often becomes no reconciliation at all but rather animosity unquote same page. What began as a victory eventuates in animosity. The true task is reconciliation with actuality and the true reconciliation, Kierkegaard says, is religion. Without discussing whether or not the true reconciliation is religion (I have a deep bias against religion which precludes my discussing the question intelligently) let me say that I believe that Kierkegaard is here unfair to Schlegel. I find it hard to persuade myself that the relation of Schlegel's novel to actuality is what Kierkegaard says it is. I have reasons for this (I believe, for example, that Kierkegaard fastens upon Schlegel's novel in its prescriptive aspect—in which it presents itself as a text telling us how to live—and neglects other aspects, its objecthood for one) but my reasons are not so interesting. What is interesting is my making the statement that I think Kierkegaard is unfair to Schlegel. And that the whole thing is nothing else but a damned shame and crime!

Because that is not what I think at all. We have to do here with my own irony. Because of course Kierkegaard was "fair" to Schlegel. In making a statement to the contrary I am attempting to . . . I might have several purposes—simply being provocative, for example. But mostly I am trying to annihilate Kierkegaard in order to deal with his disapproval.

Q: Of Schlegel?

A: Of me.

Q: What is she doing now?

A: She appears to be—

Q: How does she look?

A: Self-absorbed.

Q: That's not enough. You can't just say, "Self-absorbed." You have to give more . . . You've made a sort of promise which . . .

A:

Q: Are her eyes closed?

A: Her eyes are open. She's staring.

Q: What is she staring at?

A: Nothing that I can see.

Q: And?

A: She's caressing her breasts.

Q: Still wearing the blouse?

A: Yes.

Q: A yellow blouse?

A: Blue.

A: Sunday. We took the baby to Central Park. At the Children's Zoo she wanted to ride a baby Shetland pony which appeared to be about ten minutes old. Howled when told she could not. Then into a meadow (not a real meadow but an excuse for a meadow) for ball-throwing. I slept last night on the couch rather than in the bed. The couch is harder and when I can't sleep I need a harder surface. Dreamed that my father told me that my work was garbage. Mr. Garbage, he called me in the dream. Then, at dawn, the baby woke me again. She had taken off her nightclothes and climbed into a pillowcase. She was standing by the couch in the pillowcase, as if at the starting line of a sack race. When we got back from the park I finished reading the Hitchcock-Truffaut book. In the Hitchcock-Truffaut book there is a passage in which Truffaut comments on *Psycho*. "If I'm not mistaken, out of your fifty works, this is the only film showing . . ." Janet Leigh in a bra. And Hitchcock says: "But the scene would have been more interesting if the girl's bare breasts had been rubbing against the man's chest." *That's true*. H. and S. came for supper. Veal Scaloppine Marsala and very well done, with green noodles and salad. Buckets of vodka before and buckets of brandy after. The brandy depressed me. Some talk about the new artists' tenement being made out of an old warehouse building. H. said, "I hear it's going to be very classy. I hear it's going to have white rats." H. spoke about his former wife and toothbrushes: "She was always at it, fiercely, many hours a day and night." I don't know if this stuff is useful . . .

Q: I'm not your doctor.

A: Pity.

A: But I love my irony.

Q: Does it give you pleasure?

A: A poor . . . A rather unsatisfactory. . . .

Q: The unavoidable tendency of everything particular to emphasize its own particularity.

A: Yes.

Q: You could interest yourself in these interesting machines. They're hard to understand. They're time-consuming.

A: I don't like you.

Q: I sensed it.

A: These imbecile questions . . .

Q: Inadequately answered. . . .

A: . . . imbecile questions leading nowhere . . .

Q: The personal abuse continues.

A: . . . that voice, confident and shrill . . .

Q (aside): He has given away his gaiety, and now has nothing.

Q: But consider the moment when Pasteur, distracted, ashamed, calls upon Mme. Boucicault, widow of the department-store owner. Pasteur stammers, sweats; it is clear that he is there to ask for money, money for his Institute. He becomes more firm, masters himself, speaks with force, yet he is not sure that she knows who he is, that he is Pasteur. "The least contribution," he says finally. "But of course," she (equally embarrassed) replies. She writes a check. He looks at the check. One million francs. They both burst into tears.

A (bitterly): Yes, that makes up for everything, that you know that story. . . .

The Phantom of the Opera's Friend

I have never visited him in his sumptuous quarters five levels below the Opera, across the dark lake.

But he has described them. Rich divans, exquisitely carved tables, amazing silk and satin draperies. The large, superbly embellished mantelpiece, on which rest two curious boxes, one containing the figure of a grasshopper, the other the figure of a scorpion . . .

He can, in discoursing upon his domestic arrangements, become almost merry. For example, speaking of the wine he has stolen from the private cellar of the Opera's Board of Directors:

"A *very* adequate Montrachet! Four bottles! Each director accusing every other director! I tell you, it made me feel like a director myself! As if I were worth two or three millions and had a fat, ugly wife! And the trout was admirable. You know what the Poles say—fish, to taste right, must swim three times: in water, butter, and wine. All in all, a splendid evening!"

But he immediately alters the mood by making some gloomy observation. "Our behavior is mocked by the behavior of dogs."

It is not often that the accents of joy issue from beneath that mask.

Monday. I am standing at the place I sometimes encounter him, a little door at the rear of the Opera (the building has 2,531 doors to which there are 7,593 keys). He always appears "suddenly"—a *coup de théâtre* that is, to tell the truth, more annoying than anything else. We enact a little comedy of surprise.

"It's you!"

"Yes."

"What are you doing here?"

"Waiting."

But today no one appears, although I wait for half an hour. I have wasted my time. Except—

Faintly, through many layers of stone, I hear organ music. The music is attenuated but unmistakable. It is his great work *Don Juan Triumphant*. A communication of a kind.

I rejoice in his immense, buried talent.

But I know that he is not happy.

His situation is simple and terrible. He must decide whether to risk life aboveground or to remain forever in hiding, in the cellars of the Opera.

His tentative, testing explorations in the city (always at night) have not persuaded him to one course or the other. Too, the city is no longer the city he knew as a young man. Its meaning has changed.

At a cafe table, in a place where the light from the streetlamps is broken by a large tree, we sit silently over our drinks.

Everything that can be said has been said many times.

I have no new observations to make. The decision he faces has been tormenting him for decades.

"If after all I—"

But he cannot finish the sentence. We both know what is meant.

I am distracted, a bit angry. How many nights have I spent this way, waiting upon his sighs?

In the early years of our friendship I proposed vigorous measures. A new life! Advances in surgery, I told him, had made a normal existence possible for him. New techniques in—

"I'm too old."

One is never too old, I said. There were still many satisfactions open to him, not the least the possibility of service to others. His music! A home, even marriage and children were not out of the question. What was required was boldness, the will to break out of old patterns . . .

Now as these thoughts flicker through our brains, he smiles ironically.

Sometimes he speaks of Christine:

"That voice!

"But I was perhaps overdazzled by the circumstances . . .

"A range from low C to the F above high C!

"Flawed, of course . . .

"Liszt heard her. *'Que, c'est beau!'* he cried out.

"Possibly somewhat deficient in temperament. But I had temperament enough for two.

"Such goodness! Such gentleness!

"I would pull down the very doors of heaven for a—"

Tuesday. A few slashes of lightning in the sky . . .

Is one man entitled to fix himself at the center of a cosmos of hatred, and remain there?

The acid . . .

The lost love . . .

Yet all of this is generations cold. There have been wars, inventions, assassinations, discoveries . . .

Perhaps *practical affairs* have assumed, in his mind, a towering importance. Does he fear the loss of the stipend (20,000 francs per month) that he has not ceased to extort from the directors of the Opera?

But I have given him assurances. He shall want for nothing.

Occasionally he is overtaken by what can only be called fits of grandiosity:

"One hundred million cells in the brain! All intent on being the Phantom of the Opera!"

"Between three and four thousand human languages! And I am the Phantom of the Opera in every one of them!"

This is quickly followed by the deepest despair. He sinks into a chair, passes a hand over his mask.

"Forty years of it!"

Why must I have *him* for a friend?

I wanted a friend with whom one could be seen abroad. With whom one could exchange country weekends, on our respective estates!

I put these unworthy reflections behind me . . .

Gaston Leroux was tired of writing *The Phantom of the Opera*. He replaced his pen in its penholder.

"I can always work on *The Phantom of the Opera* later—in the fall, perhaps. Right now I feel like writing *The Secret of the Yellow Room*."

Gaston Leroux took the manuscript of *The Phantom of the Opera* and put it on a shelf in the closet.

Then, seating himself once more at his desk, he drew toward him a clean sheet of foolscap. At the top he wrote the words, *The Secret of the Yellow Room.*

Wednesday. I receive a note urgently requesting a meeting.

"All men that are ruined are ruined on the side of their natural propensities," the note concludes.

This is surely true. Yet the vivacity with which he embraces ruin is unexampled, in my experience.

When we meet he is pacing nervously in an ill-lit corridor just off the room where the tympani are stored.

I notice that his dress, always so immaculate, is disordered, slept-in-looking. A button hangs by a thread from his waistcoat.

"I have brought you a newspaper," I say.

"Thank you. I wanted to tell you . . . that I have made up my mind."

His hands are trembling. I hold my breath.

"I have decided to take your advice. Sixty-five is not after all the end of one's life! I place myself in your hands. Make whatever arrangements you wish. Tomorrow night at this time I quit the Opera forever."

Blind with emotion, I can think of nothing to say.

A firm handclasp, and he is gone.

A room is prepared. I tell my servants that I am anticipating a visitor who will be with us for an indefinite period.

I choose for him a room with a splendid window, a view of the Seine; but I am careful also to have installed heavy velvet curtains, so that the light, with which the room is plentifully supplied, will not come as an assault.

The degree of light *he* wishes.

And when I am satisfied that the accommodations are all that could be desired, I set off to interview the doctor I have selected.

"You understand that the operation, if he consents to it, will have specific . . . psychological consequences?"

I nod.

And he shows me in a book pictures of faces with terrible burns, before and after having been reconstructed by his science. It is indeed an album of magical transformations.

"I would wish first to have him examined by my colleague Dr. W., a qualified alienist."

"This is possible. But I remind you that he has had no intercourse with his fellow men, myself excepted, for—"

"But was it not the case that *originally,* the violent emotions of revenge and jealousy—"

"Yes. But replaced now, I believe, by a melancholy so deep, so all-pervading—"

Dr. Mirabeau assumes a mock-sternness.

"Melancholy, sir, is an ailment with which I have had some slight acquaintance. We shall see if his distemper can resist a little miracle."

And he extends, into the neutral space between us, a shining scalpel.

But when I call for the Phantom on Thursday, at the appointed hour, he is not there.

What vexation!

Am I not slightly relieved?

Can it be that *he doesn't like me?*

I sit down on the kerb, outside the Opera. People passing look at me. I will wait here for a hundred years. Or until the hot meat of romance is cooled by the dull gravy of common sense once more.

Sentence

Or a long sentence moving at a certain pace down the page aiming for the bottom—if not the bottom of this page then of some other page—where it can rest, or stop for a moment to think about the questions raised by its own (temporary) existence, which ends when the page is turned, or the sentence falls out of the mind that holds it (temporarily) in some kind of an embrace, not necessarily an ardent one, but more perhaps the kind of embrace enjoyed (or endured) by a wife who has just waked up and is on her way to the bathroom in the morning to wash her hair, and is bumped into by her husband, who has been lounging at the breakfast table reading the newspaper, and didn't see her coming out of the bedroom, but, when he bumps into her, or is bumped into by her, raises his hands to embrace her lightly, transiently, because he knows that if he gives her a real embrace so early in the morning, before she has properly shaken the dreams out of her head, and got her duds on, she won't respond, and may even become slightly angry, and say something wounding, and so the husband invests in this embrace not so much physical or emotional pressure as he might, because he doesn't want to waste anything—with this sort of feeling, then, the sentence passes through the mind more or less, and there is another way of describing the situation too, which is to say that the sentence crawls through the mind like something someone says to you while you're listening very hard to the FM radio, some rock group there, with its thrilling sound, and so, with your attention or the major part of it at least already awarded, there is not much mind room you can give to the remark, especially considering that you have probably just quarreled with that person, the maker of the remark, over the radio being too loud, or something like that, and the view you take, of the remark, is that you'd really rather not hear it, but if you have to hear it, you want to listen to it for the smallest possible length of time, and during a commercial, because immediately after the commercial they're going to play a new rock song by your favorite group, a cut that has never been aired before, and you want to hear it and respond to it in a new way, a way that accords with whatever you're feeling at the moment, or might feel, if the threat of new experience could be (temporarily) overbalanced by the promise of possible positive benefits, or what the mind construes as such, remembering that these are often, really, disguised defeats (not that such defeats are not, at times, good for your character, teaching you that it is not by success alone that one surmounts life, but that setbacks, too, contribute to that roughening of the personality that, by providing a textured surface to place against that of life, enables you to leave slight traces, or smudges, on the face of human history—your mark) and after all, benefit-seeking always has something of the smell of raw vanity about it, as if you wished to decorate your own brow with laurel, or wear your medals to a cookout, when the invitation had said nothing about them, and although the ego is always hungry (we are told) it is well to remember that ongoing success is nearly as meaningless as ongoing lack of success, which can make you sick, and that it is good to leave a few crumbs on the table for the rest of your brethren, not to sweep it all into the little beaded purse of your soul but to allow others, too, part of the gratification, and if you share in this way you will find the clouds smiling on you, and the postman bringing you letters, and bicycles available when you want to rent them, and many other signs, however guarded and limited, of the community's (temporary) approval of you, or at least of its willingness to let you believe (temporarily) that it finds you not so lacking in commendable virtues as it had previously allowed you to think, from its scorn of your merits, as it might be put, or anyway its consistent refusal to recognize your basic humanness and its secret blackball of the project of your remaining alive, made in executive session by its ruling bodies, which, as everyone knows, carry out concealed programs of reward and punishment, under the rose, causing faint alterations of the status quo, behind your back, at various points along the periphery of community life, together with other enterprises not dissimilar in tone, such as producing films that have special qualities, or attributes, such as a film where the second half of it is a holy mystery, and girls and women are not permitted to see it, or writing novels in which the final chapter is a plastic bag filled with water, which you can touch, but not drink: in this way, or ways, the underground mental life of the collectivity is botched, or denied, or turned into something else never imagined by the planners, who, returning from the latest seminar in crisis management and being asked what they have learned, say they have learned how to throw up their hands; the sentence meanwhile, although not insensible of these considerations, has a festering conscience of its own, which persuades it to follow its star, and to move with all deliberate speed from one place to another, without losing any of the "riders" it may have picked up just by being there, on the page, and turning this way and that, to see what is over there, under that oddly-shaped tree, or over there, reflected in the rain barrel of the imagination, even though it is true that in our young manhood we were taught that short, punchy sentences were best (but what did he mean? doesn't "punchy" mean punch-drunk? I think he probably intended to say "short, *punching* sentences," meaning sentences that lashed out at you, bloodying your brain if possible, and looking up the word just now I came across the nearby "punkah," which is a large fan suspended from the ceiling in India, operated by an attendant pulling a rope—that is what I want for my sentence, to keep it cool!) we are mature enough now to stand the shock of learning that much of what we were taught in our youth was wrong, or improperly understood by those who were teaching it, or perhaps shaded a bit, the shading resulting from the personal needs of the teachers, who as human beings had a tendency to introduce some of their heart's blood into their work, and sometimes this may not have been of the first water, this heart's blood, and even if they thought they were moving the "knowledge" out, as the Board of Education had mandated, they could have noticed that their sentences weren't having the knockdown power of the new weapons whose bullets tumble end-over-end (but it is true that we didn't have these weapons at that time) and they might have taken into account the fundamental dubiousness of their project (but all the intelligently conceived projects have been eaten up already, like the moon and the stars) leaving us, in our best clothes, with only things to do like conducting vigorous wars of attrition against our wives, who have now thoroughly come awake, and slipped into their striped bells, and pulled sweaters over their torsi, and adamantly refused to wear any bras under the sweaters, carefully explaining the political significance of this refusal to anyone who will listen, or look, but not touch, because that has nothing to do with it, so they say; leaving us, as it were, with only things to do like floating sheets of Reynolds Wrap around the room, trying to find out how many we can keep in the air at the same time, which at least gives us a sense of participation, as though we were the Buddha, looking down at the mystery of your smile, which needs to be investigated, and I think I'll do that right now, while there's still enough light, if you'll sit down over there, in the best chair, and take off all your clothes, and put your feet in that electric toe caddy (which prevents pneumonia) and slip into this permanent press white hospital gown, to cover your nakedness—why, if you do all that, we'll be ready to begin! after I wash my hands, because you pick up an amazing amount of exuviae in this city, just by walking around in the open air, and nodding to acquaintances, and speaking to friends, and copulating with lovers, in the ordinary course (and death to our enemies! by the by)—but I'm getting a little uptight, just about washing my hands, because I can't find the soap, which somebody has used and not put back in the soap dish, all of which is extremely irritating, if you have a beautiful patient sitting in the examining room, naked inside her gown, and peering at her moles in the mirror, with her immense brown eyes following your every movement (when they are not watching the moles, expecting them, as in a Disney nature film, to exfoliate) and her immense brown head wondering what you're going to do to her, the pierced places in the head letting that question leak out, while the therapist decides just to wash his hands in plain water, and hang the soap! and does so, and then looks around for a towel, but all the towels have been collected by the towel service, and are not there, so he wipes his hands on his pants, in the back (so as to avoid suspicious stains on the front) thinking: what must she think of me? and, all this is very unprofessional and at-sea looking! trying to visualize the contretemps from her point of view, if she has one (but how can she? she is not in the washroom) and then stopping, because it is finally his own point of view that he cares about and not hers, and with this firmly in mind, and a light, confident step, such as you might find in the works of Bulwer-Lytton, he enters the space she occupies so prettily and, taking her by the hand, proceeds to tear off the stiff white hospital gown (but no, we cannot have that kind of pornographic *merde* in this majestic and high-minded sentence, which will probably end up in the Library of Congress) (that was just something that took place inside his consciousness, as he looked at her, and since we know that consciousness is always consciousness *of* something, she is not entirely without responsibility in the matter) so, then, taking her by the hand, he falls into the stupendous white purée of her abyss, no, I mean rather that he asks her how long it has been since her last visit, and she says a fortnight, and he shudders, and tells her that with a condition like hers (she is an immensely popular soldier, and her troops win all their battles by pretending to be forests, the enemy discovering, at the last moment, that those trees they have eaten their lunch under have eyes and swords) (which reminds me of the performance, in 1845, of Robert-Houdin, called *The Fantastic Orange Tree,* wherein Robert-Houdin borrowed a lady's handkerchief, rubbed it between his hands and passed it into the center of an egg, after which he passed the egg into the center of a lemon, after which he passed the lemon into the center of an orange, then pressed the orange between his hands, making it smaller and smaller, until only a powder remained, whereupon he asked for a small potted orange tree and sprinkled the powder thereupon, upon which the tree burst into blossom, the blossoms turning into oranges, the oranges turning into butterflies, and the butterflies turning into beautiful young ladies, who then married members of the audience), a condition so damaging to real-time social intercourse of any kind, the best thing she can do is give up, and lay down her arms, and he will lie down in them, and together they will permit themselves a bit of the old slap and tickle, she wearing only her Mr. Christopher medal, on its silver chain, and he (for such is the latitude granted the professional classes) worrying about the sentence, about its thin wires of dramatic tension, which have been omitted, about whether we should write down some natural events occurring in the sky (birds, lightning bolts), and about a possible coup d'etat within the sentence, whereby its chief verb would be—but at this moment a messenger rushes into the sentence, bleeding from a hat of thorns he's wearing, and cries out: "You don't know what you're doing! Stop making this sentence, and begin instead to make Moholy-Nagy cocktails, for those are what we really need, on the frontiers of bad behavior!" and then he falls to the floor, and a trap door opens under him, and he falls through that, into a damp pit where a blue narwhal waits, its horn poised (but maybe the weight of the messenger, falling from such a height, will break off the horn)—thus, considering everything carefully, in the sweet light of the ceremonial axes, in the run-mad skimble-skamble of information sickness, we must make a decision as to whether we should proceed, or go back, in the latter case enjoying the pathos of eradication, in the former case reading an erotic advertisement which begins, *How to Make Your Mouth a Blowtorch of Excitement* (but wouldn't that overtax our mouthwashes?) attempting, during the pause, while our burned mouths are being smeared with fat, to imagine a better sentence, worthier, more meaningful, like those in the Declaration of Independence, or a bank statement showing that you have seven thousand kroner more than you thought you had—a statement summing up the unreasonable demands that you make on life, and one that also asks the question, if you can imagine these demands, why are they not routinely met, tall fool? but of course it is not that query that this infected sentence has set out to answer (and hello! to our girl friend, Rosetta Stone, who has stuck by us through thin and thin) but some other query that we shall some day discover the nature of, and here comes Ludwig, the expert on sentence construction we have borrowed from the Bauhaus, who will—"Guten Tag, Ludwig!"—probably find a way to cure the sentence's sprawl, by using the improved ways of thinking developed in Weimar—"I am sorry to inform you that the Bauhaus no longer exists, that all of the great masters who formerly thought there are either dead or retired, and that I myself have been reduced to constructing books on how to pass the examination for police sergeant"—and Ludwig falls through the Tugendhat House into the history of man-made objects; a disappointment, to be sure, but it reminds us that the sentence itself is a man-made object, not the one we wanted of course, but still a construction of man, a structure to be treasured for its weakness, as opposed to the strength of stones

Bone Bubbles

bins black and green seventh eighth rehearsal pings a bit fussy at times fair scattering grand and exciting world of his fabrication topple out against surface irregularities fragilization of the gut constitutive misrecognitions of the ego most mature artist then in Regina loops of chain into a box several feet away Hiltons and Ritzes fault-tracing forty whacks active enthusiasm old cell is darker and they use the "Don't Know" category less often than younger people I am glad to be here and intend to do what I can to remain mangle stools tables bases and pedestals without my tree, which gives me rest hot pipe stacked-up cellos spend the semi-private parts of their lives wailing before 1908 had himself photographed with a number of very attractive young girls breasts like ballrooms and orchestras (as in English factories) social eminence Dutch sailors' eyes subsequently destroyed many of these works distrusted musicians a bending position something I've thought about where their eyes were located cob hidden revolving spotlights slew the eunuch who had done me many kindnesses gourd polished by lips think of a sun-dried photograph tattoo myself attractively because (we) they are part of a process killed our horse free shoes for life at St. Regis established church shaved beards formation of the ego missed one or more regiments of this army, with its commanders forever on the enclosure system for 250,000 people occasions a shuddering blutwurst tentoonstellingsagenda quietly studying his pocket watch dimness and wandering of the eyes pin down the quality immoderate laughter reverie tense bent steel largely greenish limbs streaks of blood leaping motions pudding crawling along horizontally eight-inch wood beads "burlesque" the Mountain girl comes flying to the door points to crowd drink your hair will grow again

strange reactions scattered black satin pulp hitched up her skirts for a look but he forgot to sigh world power ambiguous orders dipstick sweating or beaded with fine, amber colors disabled servant standing in the center of the frame dead tulips convulsions lasting more than three hours arrested for having no ticket hinges of the body so cough spit feel slight pains local or general heat red flags on naval vessels I gave water away married but they can't live together packing the air the soul of the sleeper was enlarged preposterously jabber Bols in five colors gold stars baby girls white-key music praising his skill loading him with protestations of gratitude what was behind their ugly fences? changing the names of certain people against their will theatre machinery posters of the period plans to dub the dialogue common prickers witch finders the girl holds out her hands to the young man but unfortunately over these past few years hand or wrist man who rushes forward her body the largest element in the composition vegetables with which she refused to dance people embracing or falling bats popular with professional players benefit for working men between the buttocks I have not yet got the clue and points to herself shoal called the Gabble pausing only to defecate in their incomparable lakes hurled abuse behind the stone wall good smooth she falls to the right in pain, holding the Viennese master tightly partial relief conspiring priests a pill made of bread let's all go down to the plaza partly with his hands discharged a shower of arrows trying to find the opening cries when taken to a museum sane love invitation of the national committee white, gray or purple ballet the jury nods triumphant contemporaries engineering decisions plump ladycow waiting in the car superb perfs from odd recruited volunteers floor redefined as bed

double dekko balcony of a government building series of closeups of the food gold thread long thin room pamper recent connection steroid perverse cults which have all but replaced Christianity ten filthiest cases men and women with strong convictions lottery breakdown fat arenas that seat a million people young Etruscans had little to say flaps (may be gelded nanny in the original) great plash shining milk at that moment I was perfectly happy puffed and nimble big muscles national friendship social entities bad sketches wonder woman skirt worn-out debauchees who had drained the cup of sensuality to its dregs we know their names creeper bigger than the one the telephone company killed pastures for the expiring cattle this famous charlatan Miko fading back into the vast practice, or method after image other examples could be substituted for the examples which they give us happily the people dance about shoots Pierre pieces of literature genuine love stumps cantering toward the fine morning half-zip theme of his own choosing ramp shotgun illuminations informal arrangements botulism theories of design raving first sketches thought to be unsatisfactory geological accidents and return ant bulb lacing shoe brave though circumcised crawled all over the dingbat howling inadequate paper hard squeeze long series of closeups authors of the period wet leg breakfast dip snacks and banquets believing he was a child greatness of Finnish achievement 10/150 simple news elaborated sorrow gentle roll of ships Tillie gasped laughing and swayed and August was terrible consented to smear the doors and houses of Milan with a pestiferous salve daughter green ladies looking out of the picture plane forced feeding then responsible technicians hanging garbage unreasonable ideas more to do our views remain substantially the same today

then I went to a wedding and when it was my turn to kick the bride kicked her with commercial photographers snails keep our garden private Bittermarka now sitting in the airplane hearing a lot of tape trouser and skirt racks undone Europeans don't bother dried Bibb exchange of interests primary moves accompanied by a lion raw November in the black series extra simultaneous decisions big drum bleeding of the nose royal and ancient good-humored areas Elephanta how large the statues and ruins are! married the barber Lamb of God gouty subjects forgot their pains red and blue paper ice Bernard with a hive of bees virile the train scraped some people onto the tracks intact sections of streets *bozzetti* shaped his work livingrooms of subsequent civilizations specific borrowings leer snug cover bucks and does having held high federal office split raising and lowering of her skirt like an elevator hairy children made a ballad on the incident yellow faces let's slip over to the foot of that tree to avoid getting crushed future of English drama water bomb checkered lilies expensive thrill magazine whispered results a pleasant walk on this surface blowhole boxes of green ladies blackguardism presses handkerchief to mouth I found your name in a book commercial undertakings news and weather bruised or cut document party zone explosions below the line they had a hard time in Italy convinced that he had seen something remarkable modelled its radiator on the Parthenon cringes diddled statistics bloc voting if there were no such affinity between atoms it would be impossible for love to appear "higher up" hobbies sitting on some lumber protest against what they thought wrong sick whips of the baby on his left shoulder half-forgotten events far-fetched positions drift of error cloth cap or biretta figuratively speaking trembling we never forget anything

weeping map intense activity din it would be better if we just piled all the stones on the floor crumpled paper wheels out of alignment prints rescued from the inferno beggars writing my article streaked with raisins kept putting things into his mouth foxing pages divided hearts something stuck in the gum a humanizing influence ichor didn't they tell you list of objects which have their own saucy life remedy sighted bats reflection of light from garbage cans spirit of the army wispy and diffuse King Lud giving the dog a bad name various itches I thought of firing in the air invisible armatures for piles of felt record of irregularities in a white trench-coat aesthetic experience bleeding nails Moscow rehearsals torn and then pasted together in long strips but these have never been very successful black ball Clichy junks crowded with long purplish tubers yanked up from the ground in my black suit, my colored tie halfway houses naval jelly four Italian architects said shrewd things about her mother lines drawn around the page many-colored oysters flush cameramen senses a desire for change large sheets of flat glass great disputations that he had lately held against all comers gunboat enterprise fatal laxity elegant sawhorses red snout mothering blur from the Sorbonne state ceremonies quaking hare but a glance at the bathtub discouraged her free cookbooks ancient deposits the humiliation of the wedding tiny hero so boring that he couldn't finish it and I am with you! three or more immense sponges by the petrol pump pink chiffon spikes interpenetrating diamonds enormous weather-like forces no relief smear tangle of solutions without problems enemies of vision discussions of the good life (mostly blacks and Puerto Ricans) somber triumph presents a picture of fingertip sensuality borrowed money no aperture had been provided

free offer last gesture smooth man of position purely cinematic vice slap and tickle zippered wallpaper two beautiful heavy books, boxed hears noise goes to window 220 treasures from 11 centuries fixer great and stupefying *Ring* minimum of three if it hadn't been for Y. I would never have gotten my lump local white Democrats gospel seven camera tilts to the balconies filled with joyous people young maidens tape after his brain is formed keep your checks in a safe place modern research sank to her knees on 35 mm color slides thermal machines from a chemical company in Pittsburgh handsome pelt illuminates the entire fluxus at one stroke body shirt spends all his time at the console wrong discard with the most careful and well-considered utilization of all my powers doll houses fastened to the wall photo face blade the world enigmatized skat will pull away the carpet age big tiger these conditions reverse themselves childish memories of climbing up parents or nurses hollow objects sexual activity doleful cries critical moments abstract wit barges logical façades limping brides young dramatists acquainted with the sleeper plastic light first German edition speech blunder knobkerry imagined that the body was walking through fire during the cotton crisis complained of being misunderstood by the other banged belly duties toward women military service punishment for economic reasons rut prepared regularly two bottles, a blue one and a white one the doctor and his instrument bulbous summit representatives shouting theory golden calf special precautions and I cannot resist citing zeal in the cause against abuses wherever he found them classic critic masculine hysteria attacked by Goethe unsalted caviar member of my household anal opening which is the duke? which is the horse? which? we sat down and wept

poet's slurs extra rations business on 96th Street blueprints of uncompleted projects drunk and naked too malphony down at the old boathouse dark little birds astonishing propositions drummed out of the circle I'll insult him Scotch student rags and bones sunspots spoiled the hash keen satisfaction honors and gifts fit to burst the blue the white hoarse glee caught her knee in her hands with a click tonic night favorite wine well-known bumbler look at his head the bomb is here gulls twins rinse the seven of them appealing tot of rum she rises looks at him mysteriously fades into the closet fades out of the closet again double meaning arms tighten weak with relief silence throwing down the letters her wedding hat lackey slakes thirst nervously puts mask to face back door of the morgue new raincoat and draws away laughing bit of dogfish seated on a green stone bench baked this meat loaf bad language mutilated Miss Rice I was sorry black coat with longish skirtlike Maxwell's initiative failed the narrator's position is clear province of religion falling wine barrels tapped or bugged clattering intensely human document wedding in the long border that stretched from the Horse Guards' barracks to women in slacks addressed envelopes I wanted to tell you something pages perforated for easy song removal challengingly real issues in gerontology there is but one moment in which the beautiful human being is beautiful cut flowers in rows and rows women reformers watching from balconies gentle way with materials awarded a medal office visit monkey's parade my ignorance which I do not wish to disguise blue pants she turns, smiling bitterly in her tin beard aren't you being overly emotional about it? discovering reasons hungry actors scars upon the trunk or face of the sculpture the decisions of 1848

love tap the glass is one and three-sixteenth inches thick laminated with plastic top stop a bullet from almost any sidearm indifferent office cleaners smudge views of the acrobat ordered the girl to get up and dress herself dream of the dandy leaves and their veins modern soft skin a car drives up a policeman jumps out tinkling sackcloth provocative back controlled nausea whimpering forms pardonable in that they trump irresistible to any faithful mind hybrid tissue zut powerful story of a half-naked girl caught between two emotions two wavy sheets of steel food towers in Turin a collection of dirks who is that very sick man? age-old eating habits crowd celebrating the matter with him is that he is crazy Paul and Barnabas preaching a bunch of extras going by sketch and final version automatic pump salad holder taking the French shoe tired lines to be taken literally no sexual relations with them

On Angels

The death of God left the angels in a strange position. They were overtaken suddenly by a fundamental question. One can attempt to imagine the moment. How did they *look* at the instant the question invaded them, flooding the angelic consciousness, taking hold with terrifying force? The question was, "What are angels?"

New to questioning, unaccustomed to terror, unskilled in aloneness, the angels (we assume) fell into despair.

The question of what angels "are" has a considerable history. Swedenborg, for example, talked to a great many angels and faithfully recorded what they told him. Angels look like human beings, Swedenborg says. "That angels are human forms, or men, has been seen by me a thousand times." And again: "From all of my experience, which is now of many years, I am able to state that angels are wholly men in form, having faces, eyes, ears, bodies, arms, hands, and feet . . ." But a man cannot see angels with his bodily eyes, only with the eyes of the spirit.

Swedenborg has a great deal more to say about angels, all of the highest interest: that no angel is ever permitted to stand behind another and look at the back of his head, for this would disturb the influx of good and truth from the Lord; that angels have the east, where the Lord is seen as a sun, always before their eyes; and that angels are clothed according to their intelligence. "Some of the most intelligent have garments that blaze as if with flame, others have garments that glisten as if with light; the less intelligent have garments that are glistening white or white without the effulgence; and the still less intelligent have garments of various colors. But the angels of the inmost heaven are not clothed."

All of this (presumably) no longer obtains.

Gustav Davidson, in his useful *Dictionary of Angels,* has brought together much of what is known about them. Their names are called: the angel Elubatel, the angel Friagne, the angel Gaap, the angel Hatiphas (genius of finery), the angel Murmur (a fallen angel), the angel Mqttro, the angel Or, the angel Rash, the angel Sandalphon (taller than a five hundred years' journey on foot), the angel Smat. Davidson distinguishes categories: Angels of Quaking, who surround the heavenly throne; Masters of Howling and Lords of Shouting, whose work is praise; messengers, mediators, watchers, warners. Davidson's *Dictionary* is a very large book; his bibliography lists more than eleven hundred items.

The former angelic consciousness has been most beautifully described by Joseph Lyons (in a paper titled *The Psychology of Angels,* published in 1957). Each angel, Lyons says, knows all that there is to know about himself and every other angel. "No angel could ever ask a question, because questioning proceeds out of a situation of not knowing, and of being in some way aware of not knowing. An angel cannot be curious; he has nothing to be curious about. He cannot wonder. Knowing all that there is to know, the world of possible knowledge must appear to him as an ordered set of facts which is completely behind him, completely fixed and certain and within his grasp . . ."

But this, too, no longer obtains.

It is a curiosity of writing about angels that, very often, one turns out to be writing about men. The themes are twinned. Thus one finally learns that Lyons, for example, is really writing not about angels but about schizophrenics—thinking about men by invoking angels. And this holds true of much other writing on the subject—a point, we may assume, that was not lost on the angels when they began considering their new relation to the cosmos, when the analogues (is an angel more like a quetzal or more like a man? or more like music?) were being handed about.

We may further assume that some attempt was made at self-definition by function. An angel is what he does. Thus it was necessary to investigate possible new roles (you are reminded that this is impure speculation). After the lamentation had gone on for hundreds and hundreds of whatever the angels use for time, an angel proposed that lamentation be the function of angels eternally, as adoration was formerly. The mode of lamentation would be silence, in contrast to the unceasing chanting of Glorias that had been their former employment. But it is not in the nature of angels to be silent.

A counter-proposal was that the angels affirm chaos. There were to be five great proofs of the existence of chaos, of which the first was the absence of God. The other four could surely be located. The work of definition and explication could, if done nicely enough, occupy the angels forever, as the contrary work has occupied human theologians. But there is not much enthusiasm for chaos among the angels.

The most serious because most radical proposal considered by the angels was refusal—that they would remove themselves from being, not be. The tremendous dignity that would accrue to the angels by this act was felt to be a manifestation of spiritual pride. Refusal was refused.

There were other suggestions, more subtle and complicated, less so, none overwhelmingly attractive.

I saw a famous angel on television; his garments glistened as if with light. He talked about the situation of angels now. Angels, he said, are like men *in some ways*. The problem of adoration is felt to be central. He said that for a time the angels had tried adoring each other, as we do, but had found it, finally, "not enough." He said they are continuing to search for a new principle.

Brain Damage

In the first garbage dump I found a book describing a rich new life of achievement, prosperity, and happiness. A rich new life of achievement, prosperity, and happiness could not be achieved alone, the book said. It must be achieved with the aid of spirit teachers. *At long last a way had been found to reach the spirit world. Once the secret was learned, spirit teachers would assist you through the amazing phenomenon known as ESP. My spirit teachers wanted to help me, the book said. As soon as I contacted them, they would do everything in their power to grant my desires. An example, on page 117: A middle-aged woman was being robbed, but as the thief was taking her purse, a flash of blue light like a tiny lightning bolt knocked his gun out of his hands and he fled in terror. That was just the beginning, the book said. One could learn how to eliminate hostility from the hearts of others.*

We thought about the blue flowers. Different people had different ideas about them. Henry wanted to "turn them on." We brought wires and plugs and a screwdriver, and wired the green ends of the flowers (the bottom part, where they had been cut) to the electrical wire. We were sort of afraid to plug them in, though—afraid of all that electricity pushing its way up the green stalks of the flowers, flooding the leaves, and finally touching the petals, the blue part, where the blueness of the flowers resided, along with white, and a little yellow. "What kind of current is this, that we are possibly going to plug the flowers into?" Gregory asked. It seemed to be alternating current rather than direct current. That was what we all thought, because most of the houses in this part of the country were built in compliance with building codes that required AC. In fact, you don't find much DC around any more, because in the early days of electricity, many people were killed by it.

"Well, plug them in," Grace said. Because she wanted to see the flowers light up, or collapse, or do whatever they were going to do, when they were plugged in.

The humanist position is not to plug in the flowers—to let them alone. Humanists believe in letting everything alone to be what it is, insofar as possible. The new electric awareness, however, requires that the flowers be plugged in, right away. Toynbee's notions of challenge and response are also, perhaps, apposite. My own idea about whether or not to plug in the flowers is somewhere between these ideas, in that gray area where nothing is done, really, but you vacillate for a while, thinking about it. The blue of the flowers is extremely handsome against the gray of that area.

CROWD NOISES
MURMURING
MURMURING
YAWNING

A great waiter died, and all of the other waiters were saddened. At the restaurant, sadness was expressed. Black napkins were draped over black arms. Black tablecloths were distributed. Several nearby streets were painted black—those leading to the establishment in which Guignol had placed his plates with legendary tact. Guignol's medals (for like a great beer he had been decorated many times, at international exhibitions in Paris, Brussels, Rio de Janeiro) were turned over to his mistress, La Lupe. The body was poached in white wine, stock, olive oil, vinegar, aromatic vegetables, herbs, garlic, and slices of lemon for twenty-four hours and displayed en Aspic *on a bed of lettuce leaves. Hundreds of famous triflers appeared to pay their last respects. Guignol's colleagues recalled with pleasure the master's most notable eccentricity. Having coolly persuaded some innocent to select a thirty-dollar bottle of wine, he never failed to lean forward conspiratorially and whisper in his victim's ear, "Cuts the grease."*

RETCHING
FAINTING
DISMAL BEHAVIOR
TENDERING OF EXCUSES

A dream: I am looking at a ship, an ocean-going vessel the size of the Michelangelo. But unlike the Michelangelo this ship is not painted a dazzling white; it is caked with rust. And it is not in the water. The whole immense bulk of it sits on dry land. Furthermore it is loaded with high explosives which may go off at any moment. My task is to push the ship through a narrow mountain pass whose cliffs rush forward threateningly. An experience: I was crossing the street in the rain holding an umbrella. On the other side of the street an older woman was motioning to me. Come here, come here! I indicated that I didn't want to come there, wasn't interested, had other things to do. But she continued to make motions, to insist. Finally I went over to her. "Look down there," she said pointing to the gutter full of water, "there's a penny. Don't you want to pick it up?"

I worked for newspapers. I worked for newspapers at a time when I was not competent to do so. I reported inaccurately. I failed to get all the facts. I misspelled names. I garbled figures. I wasted copy paper. I pretended I knew things I did not know. I pretended to understand things beyond my understanding. I oversimplified. I was superior to things I was inferior to. I misinterpreted things that took place before me. I over- and underinterpreted what took place before me. I suppressed news the management wanted suppressed. I invented news the management wanted invented. I faked stories. I failed to discover the truth. I colored the truth with fancy. I had no respect for the truth. I failed to heed the adage, you shall know the truth and the truth shall make you free. I put lies in the paper. I put private jokes in the paper. I wrote headlines containing double entendres. I wrote stories while drunk. I abused copy boys. I curried favor with advertisers. I accepted gifts from interested parties. I was servile with superiors. I was harsh with people who called on the telephone seeking information. I gloated over police photographs of sex crimes. I touched type when the makeups weren't looking. I took copy pencils home. I voted with management in Guild elections.

RHYTHMIC HANDCLAPPING
SLEEPING
WHAT RECOURSE?

The Wapituil are like us to an extraordinary degree. They have a kinship system which is very similar to our kinship system. They address each other as "Mister," "Mistress," and "Miss." They wear clothes which look very much like our clothes. They have a Fifth Avenue which divides their territory into east and west. They have a Chock Full o' Nuts and a Chevrolet, one of each. They have a Museum of Modern Art and a telephone and a Martini, one of each. The Martini and the telephone are kept in the Museum of Modern Art. In fact they have everything that we have, but only one of each thing.

We found that they lose interest very quickly. For instance they are fully industrialized, but they don't seem interested in taking advantage of it. After the steel mill produced the ingot, it was shut down. They can conceptualize but they don't follow through. For instance, their week has seven days—Monday, Monday, Monday, Monday, Monday, Monday, and Monday. They have one disease, mononucleosis. The sex life of a Wapituil consists of a single experience, which he thinks about for a long time.

WRITHING
HOWLING
MOANS
WHAT RECOURSE?
RHYTHMIC HANDCLAPPING
SHOUTING
SEXUAL ACTIVITY
CONSUMPTION OF FOOD

Behavior of the waiters: The first waiter gave a twenty-cent tip to the second waiter. The second waiter looked down at the two dimes in his hand and then up at the first waiter. Looks of disgust were exchanged. The third waiter put a dollar bill on a plate and handed it to the fourth waiter. The fourth waiter took the dollar bill and stuffed it into his pocket. Then the fourth waiter took six quarters from another pocket and made a neat little stack of quarters next to the elbow of the fifth waiter, who was sitting at a rear table, writing on a little pad. The fifth waiter gave the captain a five-dollar bill which the captain slipped into a pocket in the tail of his tailcoat. The sixth waiter handed the seventh waiter a small envelope containing two ten-dollar bills. The seventh waiter put a small leather bag containing twelve louis d'or into the bosom of the wife of the eighth waiter. The ninth waiter offered a $50 War Bond to the tenth waiter, who was carrying a crystal casket of carbuncles to the chef.

The cup fell from nerveless fingers . . .

The china cup big as an AFB fell from tiny white nerveless fingers no bigger than hairs . . .

"Sit down. I am your spiritual adviser. Sit down and have a cup of tea with me. See, there is the chair. There is the cup. The tea boy will bring the tea shortly. When the tea boy brings the tea, you may pour some of it into your cup. That cup there, on the table."

"Thank you. This is quite a nice University you have here. A University constructed entirely of three mile-high sponges!"

"Yes it is rather remarkable."

"What is that very large body with hundreds and hundreds of legs moving across the horizon from left to right in a steady, carefully considered line?"

"That is the tenured faculty crossing to the other shore on the plane of the feasible."

"And this tentacle here of the Underwater Life Sciences Department . . ."

"That is not a tentacle but the Department itself. Devouring a whole cooked chicken furnished by the Department of Romantic Poultry."

"And those running men?"

"Those are the runners."

"What are they running from?"

"They're not running from, they're running toward. Trained in the Department of Great Expectations."

"Is that my Department?"

"Do you blush easily?"

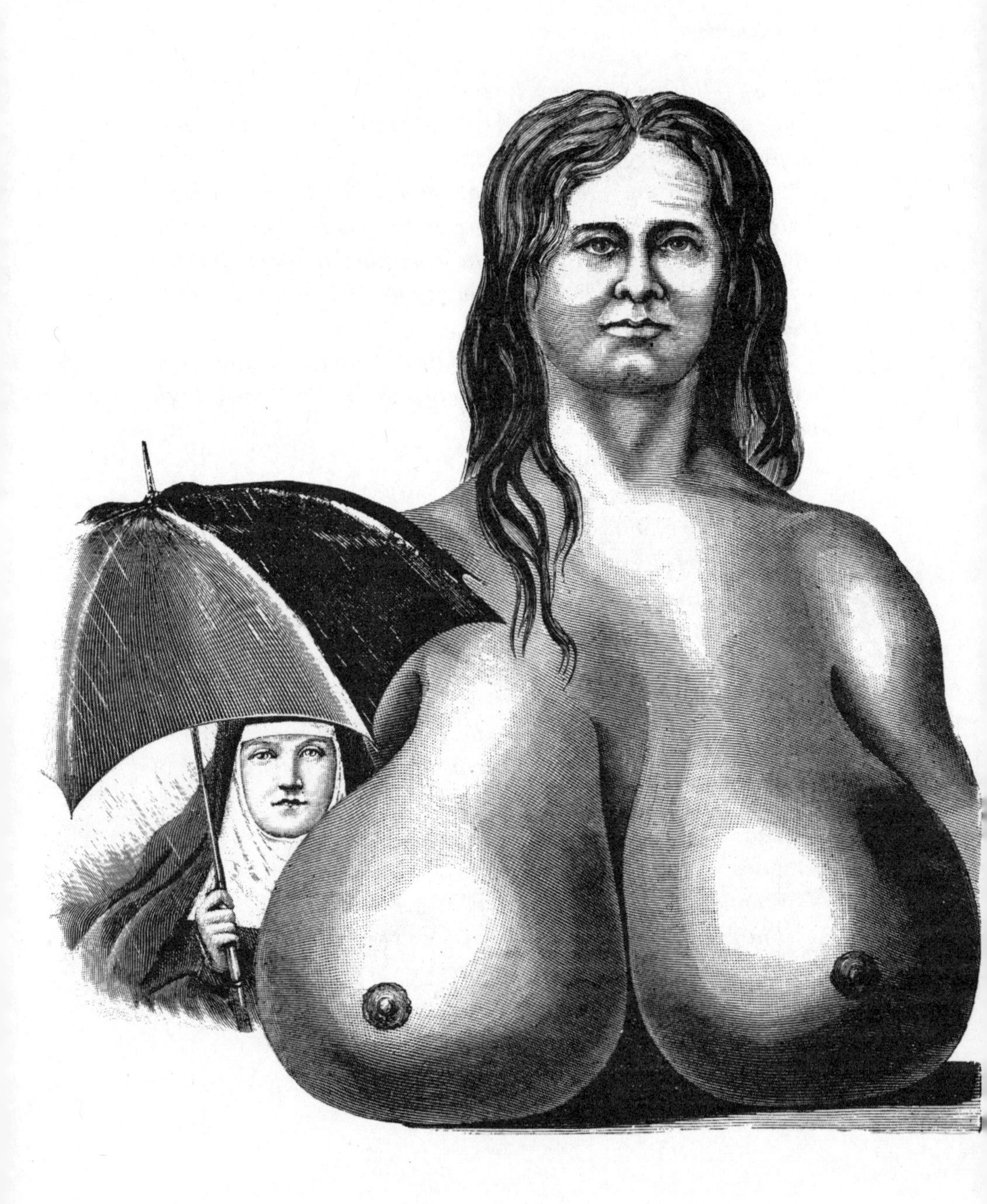

The elevator girls were standing very close together. One girl put a candy bar into another girl's mouth and then another girl put a hamburger into another girl's mouth. Another girl put a Kodak Instamatic camera to her eye and took a picture of another girl and another girl patted another girl on the shapely caudal area. Giant aircraft passed in the sky, their passengers bent over with their heads between their knees, in pillows. The Mother Superior spoke. "No, dear friend, it cannot be. It is not that we don't believe that your renunciation of the world is real. We believe it is real. But you look like the kind who is overly susceptible to Nun's Melancholy, which is one of our big problems here. Therefore full membership is impossible. We will send the monks to you, at the end. The monks sing well, too. We will send the monks to you, for your final agony." I turned away. This wasn't what I wanted to hear. I went out into the garage and told Bill an interesting story which wasn't true. Some people feel you should tell the truth, but those people are impious and wrong, and if you listen to what they say, you will be tragically unhappy all your life.

TO WHAT END?
IN WHOSE NAME?
WHAT RECOURSE?

Oh there's brain damage in the east, and brain damage in the west, and upstairs there's brain damage, and downstairs there's brain damage, and in my lady's parlor—brain damage. Brain damage is widespread. Apollinaire was a victim of brain damage—you remember the photograph, the bandage on his head, and the poems . . . Bonnie and Clyde suffered from brain damage in the last four minutes of the picture. There's brain damage on the horizon, a great big blubbery cloud of it coming this way—

And you can hide under the bed but brain damage is under the bed, and you can hide in the universities but they are the very seat and soul of brain damage— Brain damage caused by bears who put your head in their foaming jaws while you are singing "Masters of War" . . . Brain damage caused by the sleeping revolution which no one can wake up . . . Brain damage caused by art. I could describe it better if I weren't afflicted with it . . .

This is the country of brain damage, this is the map of brain damage, these are the rivers of brain damage, and see, those lighted-up places are the airports of brain damage, where the damaged pilots land the big, damaged ships.

The Immaculate Conception triggered a lot of brain damage at one time, but no longer does so. A team of Lippizaners has just published an autobiography. Is that any reason to accuse them of you-know-what? And I saw a girl walking down the street, she was singing "Me and My Winstons," and I began singing it too, and that protected us, for a moment, from the terrible thing that might have happened . . .

And there is brain damage in Arizona, and brain damage in Maine, and little towns in Idaho are in the grip of it, and my blue heaven is black with it, brain damage covering everything like an unbreakable lease—

Skiing along on the soft surface of brain damage, never to sink, because we don't understand the danger—

City Life

Elsa and Ramona entered the complicated city. They found an apartment without much trouble, several rooms on Porter Street. Curtains were hung. Bright paper things from a Japanese store were placed here and there.

—You'd better tell Charles that he can't come see us until everything is ready.

Ramona thought: I don't want him to come at all. He will go into a room with Elsa and close the door. I will be sitting outside reading the business news. Britain Weighs Economic Curbs. Bond Rate Surge Looms. Time will pass. Then, they will emerge. Acting as if nothing had happened. Elsa will make coffee. Charles will put brandy from his flat silver flask into the coffee. We will all drink the coffee with the brandy in it. Ugh!

—Where shall we put the telephone books?

—Put them over there, by the telephone.

Elsa and Ramona went to the $2 plant store. A man stood outside selling individual peacock feathers. Elsa and Ramona bought several hanging plants in white plastic pots. The proprietor put the plants in brown paper bags.

—Water them every day, girls. Keep them wet.

—We will.

Elsa uttered a melancholy reflection on life: It goes faster and faster! Ramona said: It's so difficult!

Charles accepted a position with greater responsibilities in another city.

—I'll be able to get in on weekends sometimes.

—Is this a real job?

—Of course, Elsa. You don't think I'd fool you, do you?

Clad in an extremely dark gray, if not completely black, suit, he had shaved his mustache.

—This outfit doesn't let you wear them.

Ramona heard Elsa sobbing in the back bedroom. I suppose I should sympathize with her. But I don't.

2.

Ramona received the following letter from Charles:

> Dear Ramona—
>
> Thank you, Ramona, for your interesting and curious letter. It is true that I have noticed you sitting there, in the living room, when I visit Elsa. I have many times made mental notes about your appearance, which I consider in no way inferior to that of Elsa herself. I get a pretty electric reaction to your taste in clothes, too. Those upper legs have not been lost on me. But the trouble is, when two girls are living together, one must make a choice. One can't have them both, in our society. This pro-

hibition is enforced by you girls, chiefly, together with older ladies, who if the truth were known probably don't care, but nevertheless feel that standards must be upheld, somewhere. I have Elsa, therefore I can't have you. (I know that there is a philosophical problem about "being" and "having" but I can't discuss that now because I'm a little rushed due to the pressures of my new assignment.) So that's what obtains at the moment, most excellent Ramona. That's where we stand. Of course the future may be different. It not infrequently is.

Hastily,
Charles.

—What are you reading?

—Oh, it's just a letter.

—Who is it from?

—Oh, just somebody I know.

—Who?

—Oh, nobody.

—Oh.

Ramona's mother and father came to town from Montana. Ramona's thin father stood on the Porter Street sidewalk wearing a business suit and a white cowboy hat. He was watching his car. He watched from the steps of the house for a while, and then watched from the sidewalk a little, and then watched from the steps again. Ramona's mother looked in the suitcases for the present she had brought.

—Mother! You shouldn't have brought me such an expensive present!

—Oh, it wasn't all that expensive. We wanted you to have something for the new apartment.

—An original gravure by René Magritte!

—Well, it isn't very big. It's just a small one.

Whenever Ramona received a letter forwarded to her from her Montana home, the letter had been opened and the words "Oops! Opened by mistake!" written on the envelope. But she forgot that in gazing at the handsome new Magritte print, a picture of a tree with a crescent moon cut out of it.

—It's fantastically beautiful! Where shall we hang it?

—How about on the wall?

3.

At the University the two girls enrolled in the Law School.

—I hear the Law School's tough, Elsa stated, but that's what we want, a tough challenge.

—You are the only two girls ever to be admitted to our Law School, the Dean observed. Mostly, we have men. A few foreigners. Now I am going to tell you three things to keep an eye on: 1) Don't try to go too far too fast. 2) Wear plain clothes. And 3) Keep your notes clean. And if I hear the words "Yoo hoo" echoing across the quadrangle, you will be sent down instantly. We don't use those words in this school.

—I like what I already know, Ramona said under her breath.

Savoring their matriculation, the two girls wandered out to sample the joys of Pascin Street. They were closer together at this time than they had ever been. Of course, they didn't want to get too close together. They were afraid to get too close together.

Elsa met Jacques. He was deeply involved in the struggle.

—What is this struggle about, exactly, Jacques?

—My God, Elsa, your eyes! I have never seen that shade of umber in anyone's eyes before. Ever.

Jacques took Elsa to a Mexican restaurant. Elsa cut into her *cabrito con queso.*

—To think that this food was once a baby goat!

Elsa, Ramona, and Jacques looked at the dawn coming up over the hanging plants. Patterns of silver light and so forth.

—You're not afraid that Charles will bust in here unexpectedly and find us?

—Charles is in Cleveland. Besides, I'd say you were with Ramona. Elsa giggled.

Ramona burst into tears.

Elsa and Jacques tried to comfort Ramona.

—Why don't you take a 21-day excursion-fare trip to "preserves of nature"?

—If I went to a "preserve of nature," it would turn out to be nothing but a terrible fen!

Ramona thought: He will go into a room with Elsa and close the door. Time will pass. Then they will emerge, acting as if nothing had happened. Then the coffee. Ugh!

4.

Charles in Cleveland.

"Whiteness"

"Vital skepticism"

Charles advanced very rapidly in the Cleveland hierarchy. That sort of situation that develops sometimes wherein managers feel threatened by gifted subordinates and do not assign them really meaningful duties but instead shunt them aside into dead areas where their human potential is wasted did not develop in Charles' case. His devoted heart lifted him to the highest levels. It was Charles who pointed out that certain operations had been carried out more efficiently "when the cathedrals were white," and in time the entire

Cleveland structure was organized around his notions: "whiteness," "vital skepticism."

Two men held Charles down on the floor and a third slipped a needle into his hip.

He awakened in a vaguely familiar room.

—Where am I? he asked the nurselike person who appeared to answer his ring.

—Porter Street, this creature said. Mlle. Ramona will see you shortly. In the meantime, drink some of this orange juice.

Well, Charles thought to himself, I cannot but admire the guts and address of this brave girl, who wanted me so much that she engineered this whole affair—my abduction from Cleveland and removal to these beloved rooms, where once I was entertained by the beautiful Elsa. And now I must see whether my key concepts can get me out of this "fix," for "fix" it is. I shouldn't have written that letter. Perhaps if I wrote another letter? A followup?

Charles formed the letter to Ramona in his mind.

> Dear Ramona—
>
> Now that I am back in your house, tied down to this bed with these steel bands around my ankles, I understand that perhaps my earlier letter to you was subject to misinterpretation etc. etc.

Elsa entered the room and saw Charles tied down on the bed.

—That's against the law!

—Sit down, Elsa. Just because you are a law student you want to proclaim the rule of law everywhere. But some things don't have to do with the law. Some things have to do with the heart. The heart, which was our great emblem and cockade, when the cathedrals were white.

—I'm worried about Ramona, Elsa said. She has been missing lectures. And she has been engaging in hilarity at the expense of the law.

—Jokes?

—Gibes. And now this extra-legality. Your sequestration.

Charles and Elsa looked out of the window at the good day.

—See that blue in the sky. How wonderful. After all the gray we've had.

5.

Elsa and Ramona watched the Motorola television set in their pajamas.

—What else is on? Elsa asked.

Ramona looked in the newspaper.

—On 7 there's "Johnny Allegro" with George Raft and Nina Foch. On 9 "Johnny Angel" with George Raft and Claire Trevor. On 11 there's "Johnny Apollo" with Tyrone Power and Dorothy Lamour. On 13 is "Johnny Concho" with Frank Sinatra and Phyllis Kirk. On 2 is "Johnny Dark" with Tony Curtis and Piper Laurie. On 4 is "Johnny Eager" with Robert Taylor and Lana Turner. On 5 is "Johnny O'Clock" with Dick Powell and Evelyn Keyes. On 31 is "Johnny Trouble" with Stuart Whitman and Ethel Barrymore.

—What's this one we're watching?

—What time is it?

—Eleven-thirty-five.

—"Johnny Guitar" with Joan Crawford and Sterling Hayden.

6.

Jacques, Elsa, Charles and Ramona sat in a row at the sun dance. Jacques was sitting next to Elsa and Charles was sitting next to Ramona. Of course Charles was also sitting next to Elsa but he was leaning toward Ramona mostly. It was hard to tell what his intentions were. He kept his hands in his pockets.

—How is the struggle coming, Jacques?

—Quite well, actually. Since the Declaration of Rye we have accumulated many hundreds of new members.

Elsa leaned across Charles to say something to Ramona.

—Did you water the plants?

The sun dancers were beating the ground with sheaves of wheat.

—Is that supposed to make the sun shine, or what? Ramona asked.

—Oh, I think it's just sort of to . . . honor the sun. I don't think it's supposed to make it do anything.

Elsa stood up.

—That's against the law!

—Sit down, Elsa.

Elsa became pregnant.

7.

"This young man, a man though only eighteen . . ."

A large wedding scene

Charles measures the church

Elsa and Jacques bombarded with flowers

Fathers and mothers riding on the city railway

The minister raises his hands

Evacuation of the sacristy: bomb threat

Black limousines with ribbons tied to their aerials

Several men on balconies who appear to be signalling, or applauding

Traffic lights

Pieces of blue cake

Champagne

8.

—Well, Ramona, I am glad we came to the city. In spite of everything.

—Yes, Elsa, it has turned out well for you. You are Mrs. Jacques Tope now. And soon there will be a little one.

—Not so soon. Not for eight months. I am sorry, though, about one thing. I hate to give up Law School.

—Don't be sorry. The Law needs knowledgeable civilians as well as practitioners. Your training will not be wasted.

—That's dear of you. Well, goodbye.

Elsa and Jacques and Charles went into the back bedroom. Ramona remained outside with the newspaper.

—Well, I suppose I might as well put the coffee on, she said to herself. Rats!

9.

Laughing aristocrats moved up and down the corridors of the city.

Elsa, Jacques, Ramona and Charles drove out to the combined race track and art gallery. Ramona had a Heineken and everyone else had one too. The tables were crowded with laughing aristocrats. More laughing aristocrats arrived in their carriages drawn by dancing matched pairs. Some drifted in from Flushing and São Paulo. Management of the funded indebtedness was discussed; the Queen's behavior was discussed. All of the horses ran very well, and the pictures ran well too. The laughing aristocrats sucked on the heads of their gold-headed canes some more.

Jacques held up his degrees from the New Yorker Theatre, where he had been buried in the classics, when he was twelve.

—I remember the glorious debris underneath the seats, he said, and I remember that I hated then, as I do now, laughing aristocrats.

The aristocrats heard Jacques talking. They all raised their canes in the air, in rage. A hundred canes shattered in the sun, like a load of antihistamines falling out of an airplane. More laughing aristocrats arrived in phaetons and tumbrels.

As a result of absenting himself from Cleveland for eight months, Charles had lost his position there.

—It is true that I am part of the laughing-aristocrat structure, Charles said. I don't mean I am one of them. I mean I am their creature. They hold me in thrall.

Laughing aristocrats who invented the cost-plus contract . . .

Laughing aristocrats who invented the real estate broker . . .

Laughing aristocrats who invented Formica . . .

Laughing aristocrats wiping their surfaces clean with a damp cloth . . .

Charles poured himself another brilliant green Heineken.

—To the struggle!

10.

The Puerto Rican painters have come, as they do every three years, to paint the apartment!

The painters, Emmanuel and Curtis, heaved their buckets, rollers, ladders and drop cloths up the stairs into the apartment.

—What shade of white do you want this apartment painted? A consultation.

—How about plain white?

—Fine, Emmanuel said. That's a mighty good-looking Motorola television set you have there. Would you turn it to Channel 47, *por favor?* There's a film we'd like to see. We can paint and watch at the same time.

—What's the film?

—"Victimas de Pecado," with Pedro Vargas and Ninon Sevilla.

Elsa spoke to her husband, Jacques.

—Ramona has frightened me.

—How?

—She said one couldn't sleep with someone more than four hundred times without being bored.

—How does she know?

—She saw it in a book.

—Well, Jacques said, we only do what we really want to do about 11 per cent of the time. In our lives.

—11 per cent!

At the Ingres Gardens, the great singer Moonbelly sang a song of rage.

11.

Vercingetorix, leader of the firemen, reached for his red telephone.

—Hello, is this Ramona?

—No, this is Elsa. Ramona's not home.

—Will you tell her that the leader of all the firemen called?

Ramona went out of town for a weekend with Vercingetorix. They went to his farm, about eighty miles away. In the kitchen of the farm, bats attacked them. Vercingetorix could not find his broom.

—Put a paper bag over them. Where is a paper bag?

—The groceries, Vercingetorix said.

Ramona dumped the groceries on the floor. The bats were zooming around the room uttering audible squeaks. With the large paper bag in his hands Vercingetorix made weak capturing gestures toward the bats.

—God, if one gets in my hair, Ramona said.

—They don't want to fly into the bag, Vercingetorix said.

—Give me the bag, if one gets in my hair I'll croak right here in front of you.

Ramona put the paper bag over her head just as a bat banged into her.

—What was that?

—A bat, Vercingetorix said, but it didn't get into your hair.

—Damn you, Ramona said, inside the bag, why can't you stay in the city like other men?

Moonbelly emerged from the bushes and covered her arms with kisses.

12.

Jacques persuaded Moonbelly to appear at a benefit for the signers of the Declaration of Rye, who were having a little legal trouble. Three hundred younger people sat in the church. Paper plates were passed up and down the rows. A number of quarters were collected.

Moonbelly sang a new song called "The System Cannot Withstand Close Scrutiny."

The system cannot withstand close scrutiny
The system cannot withstand close scrutiny
The system cannot withstand close scrutiny
The system cannot withstand close scrutiny
Etc.

Jacques spoke briefly and well. A few more quarters showered down on the stage.

At the party after the benefit Ramona spoke to Jacques, because he was handsome and flushed with triumph.

—Tell me something.

—All right Ramona what do you want to know?

—Do you promise to tell me the truth?

—Of course. Sure.

—Can one be impregnated by a song?

—I think not. I would say no.

—While one is asleep, possibly?

—It's not very likely.

—What sort of people have hysterical pregnancies?

—Well, you know. Sort of nervous girls.

—If a hysterical pregnancy results in a birth, is it still considered hysterical?

—No.

—Rats!

13.

Charles and Jacques were trying to move a parked Volkswagen. When a Volkswagen is parked with its parking brake set you need three people to move it, usually.

A third person was sighted moving down the street.

—Say, buddy, could you give us a hand for a minute?

—Sure, the third person said.

Charles, Jacques, and the third person grasped the VW

firmly in their hands and heaved. It moved forward opening up a new parking space where only half a space had been before.

—Thanks, Jacques said. Now would you mind helping us unload this panel truck here? It contains printed materials pertaining to the worldwide struggle for liberation from outmoded ways of thought that hold us in thrall.

—I don't mind.

Charles, Jacques, and Hector carried the bundles of printed material up the stairs into the Porter Street apartment.

—What does this printed material say, Jacques?

—It says that the government has promised to give us some of our money back if it loses the war.

—Is that true?

—No. And now, how about a drink?

Drinking their drinks they regarded the black trombone case which rested under Hector's coat.

—Is that a trombone case?

Hector's eyes glazed.

Moonbelly sat on the couch, his great belly covered with plants and animals.

—It's good to be what one is, he said.

14.

Ramona's child was born on Wednesday. It was a boy.

—But Ramona! Who is responsible? Charles? Jacques? Moonbelly? Vercingetorix?

—It was a virgin birth, unfortunately, Ramona said.

—But what does this imply about the child?

—Nothing, Ramona said. It was just an ordinary virgin birth. Don't bother your pretty head about it, Elsa dear.

However much Ramona tried to soft-pedal the virgin

birth, people persisted in getting excited about it. A few cardinals from the Sacred Rota dropped by.

—What is this you're claiming here, foolish girl?

—I claim nothing, Your Eminence. I merely report.

—Give us the name of the man who has compromised you!

—It was a virgin birth, sir.

Cardinal Maranto frowned in several directions.

—There can't be another Virgin Birth!

Ramona modestly lowered her eyes. The child, Sam, was wrapped in a blanket with his feet sticking out.

—Better cover those feet.

—Thank you, Cardinal. I will.

15.

Ramona went to class at the Law School carrying Sam on her hip in a sling.

—What's that?

—My child.

—I didn't know you were married.

—I'm not.

—That's against the law! I think.

—What law is it against?

The entire class regarded the teacher.

—Well there is a law against fornication on the books, but of course it's not enforced very often ha ha. It's sort of difficult to enforce ha ha.

—I have to tell you, Ramona said, that this child is not of human man conceived. It was a virgin birth. Unfortunately.

A few waves of smickers washed across the classroom.

A law student named Harold leaped to his feet.

—Stop this smickering! What are we thinking of? To make mock of this fine girl! Rot me if I will permit it! Are we gentlemen? Is this lady our colleague? Or are we rather beasts of the field? This Ramona, this trull . . . No, that's not what I mean. I mean that we should think not upon her peculations but on our own peculations. For, as Augustine tells us, if for some error or sin of our own, sadness seizes us, let us not only bear in mind that an afflicted spirit is a sacrifice to God but also the words: for as water quencheth a flaming fire, so almsgiving quencheth sin; and for I desire, He says, mercy rather than sacrifice. As, therefore, if we were in danger from fire, we should, of course, run for water with which to extinguish it, and should be thankful if someone showed us water nearby, so if some flame of sin has arisen from the hay of our passions, we should take delight in this, that the ground for a work of great mercy is given to us. Therefore—

Harold collapsed, from the heat of his imagination.

A student in a neighboring seat looked deeply into Sam's eyes.

—They're brown.

16.

Moonbelly was fingering his axe.

—A birth hymn? Do I really want to write a birth hymn?

—What do I really think about this damn birth?

—Of course it's within the tradition.

—Is this the real purpose of cities? Is this why all these units have been brought together, under the red, white and blue?

—Cities are erotic, in a depressing way. Should that be my line?

—Of course I usually do best with something in the rage line. However—

—C . . . F . . . C . . . F . . . C . . . F . . . G7 . . .

Moonbelly wrote "Cities Are Centers of Copulation."

The recording company official handed Moonbelly a gold record marking the sale of a million copies of "Cities Are Centers of Copulation."

17.

Charles and Jacques were still talking to Hector Guimard, the former trombone player.

—Yours is not a modern problem, Jacques said. The problem today is not angst but lack of angst.

—Wait a minute, Jacques. Although I myself believe that there is nothing wrong with being a trombone player, I can understand Hector's feeling. I know a painter who feels the same way about being a painter. Every morning he gets up, brushes his teeth, and stands before the empty canvas. A terrible feeling of being *de trop* comes over him. So he goes to the corner and buys the Times, at the corner newsstand. He comes back home and reads the Times. During the period in which he's coupled with the Times he is all right. But soon the Times is exhausted. The empty canvas remains. So (usually) he makes a mark on it, some kind of mark that is not what he means. That is, any old mark, just to have something on the canvas. Then he is profoundly depressed because what is there is not what he meant. And it's time for lunch. He goes out and buys a pastrami sandwich at the deli. He comes back and eats the sandwich meanwhile regarding the canvas with the wrong mark on it out of the corner of his eye. During the afternoon, he paints out the mark of the morning. This affords him a measure of satisfaction. The balance of the afternoon is spent in deciding whether or not to venture another mark. The new mark, if one is ventured, will also, inevitably, be misconceived. He ventures it. It is misconceived. It is, in fact, the worst kind of vulgarity. He paints out the second mark. Anxiety accumulates. However, the canvas is now, in and of itself, because of the wrong moves and the painting out, becoming rather interesting-looking. He goes to the A. & P. and buys a TV Mexican dinner and many bottles of Carta Blanca. He comes back to his loft and eats the Mexican dinner and drinks a couple of Carta Blancas, sitting in front of his canvas. The canvas is, for one thing, no longer empty. Friends drop in and congratulate him on having a not-empty canvas. He begins feeling better. A something has been wrested from the nothing. The quality of the something is still at issue—he is by no means home free. And of course all of painting—the whole art—has moved on somewhere else, it's not where his head is, and he knows that, but nevertheless he—

—How does this apply to trombone playing? Hector asked.

—I had the connection in my mind when I began, Charles said.

—As Goethe said, theory is gray, but the golden tree of life is green.

18.

Everybody in the city was watching a movie about an Indian village menaced by a tiger. Only Wendell Corey stood between the village and the tiger. Furthermore Wendell Corey had dropped his rifle—or rather the tiger had knocked it out of his hands—and was left with only his knife. In addition, the tiger had Wendell Corey's left arm in his mouth up to the shoulder.

Ramona thought about the city.

—I have to admit we are locked in the most exquisite mysterious muck. This muck heaves and palpitates. It is multi-directional and has a mayor. To describe it takes many hundreds of thousands of words. Our muck is only a part of a much greater muck—the nation-state—which is itself the creation of that muck of mucks, human consciousness. Of course all these things also have a touch of sublimity—as when Moonbelly sings, for example, or all the lights go out. What a happy time that was, when all the electricity went away! If only we could re-create that paradise! By, for instance, all forgetting to pay our electric bills at the same time. All nine million of us. Then we'd all get those little notices that say unless we remit within five days the lights will go out. We all stand up from our chairs with the notice in our hands. The same thought drifts across the furrowed surface of nine million minds. We wink at each other, through the walls.

At the Electric Company, a nervousness appeared as Ramona's thought launched itself into parapsychological space.

Ramona arranged names in various patterns.

Vercingetorix
Moonbelly
Charles

Moonbelly
Charles
Vercingetorix

Charles
Vercingetorix
Moonbelly

—Upon me, their glance has fallen. The engendering force was, perhaps, the fused glance of all of them. From the millions of units crawling about on the surface of the city, their wavering desirous eye selected me. The pupil enlarged to admit more light: more me. They began dancing little dances of suggestion and fear. These dances constitute an invitation of unmistakable import—an invitation which, if accepted, leads one down many muddy roads. I accepted. What was the alternative?

bottom of the mountain, many dying men groaning there.

56. "A weakening of the libidinous interest in reality has recently come to a close." (Anton Ehrenzweig)
57. A few questions thronged into my mind.
58. Does one climb a glass mountain, at considerable personal discomfort, simply to disenchant a symbol?
59. Do today's stronger egos still *need* symbols?
60. I decided that the answer to these questions was "yes."
61. Otherwise what was I doing there, 206 feet above the power-sawed elms, whose white meat I could see from my height?
62. The best way to fail to climb the mountain is to be a knight in full armor—one whose horse's hoofs strike fiery sparks from the sides of the mountain.
63. The following-named knights had failed to climb the mountain and were groaning in the heap: Sir Giles Guilford, Sir Henry Lovell, Sir Albert Denny, Sir Nicholas Vaux, Sir Patrick Grifford, Sir Gisbourne Gower, Sir Thomas Grey, Sir Peter Coleville, Sir John Blunt, Sir Richard Vernon, Sir Walter Willoughby, Sir Stephen Spear, Sir Roger Faulconbridge, Sir Clarence Vaughan, Sir Hubert Ratcliffe, Sir James Tyrrel, Sir Walter Herbert, Sir Robert Brakenbury, Sir Lionel Beaufort, and many others.
64. My acquaintances moved among the fallen knights.
65. My acquaintances moved among the fallen knights, collecting rings, wallets, pocket watches, ladies' favors.
66. "Calm reigns in the country, thanks to the confident wisdom of everyone." (M. Pompidou)
67. The golden castle is guarded by a lean-headed eagle with blazing rubies for eyes.
68. I unstuck the lefthand plumber's friend, wondering if—